# EXTRATERRESTRIAL
# SPEAK
# PART TEN

# EXTRATERRESTRIAL
# SPEAK
# PART TEN

Lou Baldin

EXTRATERRESTRIAL SPEAK PART TEN



ISBN: 9798666633175

Imprint: Independently published

This book contains discussions, questions, and answers, from Baldin.proboards.com.

From February 15, 2011, to June 5, 2011.

Some questions and answers were edited for clarification by Lou Baldin

### **TEXT NOTES:**

1) Regular text = Questions by ProBoard members

2) **Bold text =** Answers by Lou

3) *Italic text = Quotes by Lou within members Question*

4) Forum member name removed = [nnnn] except the comical banter between Lou & John Lear)

**"Pg.." designates page numbers on thread <u>Questions and comments for Sleeper/Lou</u> from http://baldin.proboards.com/**

Contents

Q:  Lou said: *"Not Milton's ancestor.  There is some truth to the story, none of which is pleasing to human eyes and ears."*  Why isn't it pleasing to human eyes and ears?  Are beings like that against us humans?

**A:  There are a good number of beings against humans, some we even vote for because of their fake charm and deceptive smiles.**

Q:  Hey Lou Good morning!  As technology advances in video and picture cameras, are we going to be able to see more UFO / paranormal stuff?  Thanks!!

**A:  A bit, but proving non-human origin is a debunker's trump card.  By design.**

Q:  Hi Lou, I saw this video in which they were describing actual technology they have.  One example was of these microchips the size of dust particles.  Apparently, they can spread them around like dust and it makes it possible for GPS navigation anywhere in the world.  Their idea was so that in the future people wouldn't have to drive vehicles, or planes.  They would drive themselves and navigate via these tiny microchips.  Then I got to thinking that maybe that's what the chemtrails are.  What do you think?

**A:  You mean vapor trails.  That is not how it goes down.**

Q:  Hello Sleeper, I have been listening to the forward of "The Book of Urantia".  I have only been able to listen to the audio file of the forward of this book.  The damned thing is just too complex and big to listen to and I just don't have the time to read it.  I usually fall asleep while listening to it at night.  I usually take falling asleep while listening or reading as a sign as "good info" for some reason.

The question I have is, this Book came up around the Age of Aquarius around the 60's.  Is this a new stage or prop of a future religion?  If you take the time to take a look at this book here:

 It was supposed to have been made by a group of people tasked with the charge of using the symbol of the English language to the best of their ability to convey a message. From just the forward a lot of things coincide with your info.

Have you come across this Book before Sleeper?  Can Milton tell you a little about its faction or anything?

**A:  People have mentioned that book on this site and ATS, but I haven't' taken the time to read it.  Milton hasn't either.**

# Pg. 443— 2011-02-16

Q:  Lou, I'm interested about suicide and how it relates to graduation.  I understand the aspects of this 3D dreamland we live in; does suicide negate graduation?

**A:  Suicide is judged individually.  Best have a good reason to do it.  The consequences can be horrific; the lucky ones get sent back for another try.  FYI, MOST reasons are "not" acceptable!**

Q:  Hi Sleeper/Lou and everyone, this is my first post.  At last, after reading through more than 400 pages, I hope this is not a repeat question: Sleeper, can you shed some light on the Sator square?

"The Sator Square is a word square containing a Latin palindrome featuring the words: SATOR AREPO TENET OPERA ROTAS written in a square so that they may be read top-to-bottom, bottom-to-top, left-to-right, and right-to-left.  The earliest known appearance of the square was found in the ruins of Pompeii which was buried in the ash of Mt.  Vesuvius in 79 AD."  (from Wikipedia)

A few things can be gleaned from the individual words.  SATOR means sower, planter, originator.  AREPO could mean 'creep towards', or it could be a somebody's name.  TENET means to hold, preserve, rule.  OPERA is work, labor.  ROTAS translates to wheel or rotate.

My own poor translation = 'the sower Arepo preserves those who labor in a constant cycle'.  It sort of describes those on this rock.  It certainly describes my locale, a third world country trying to maintain the illusion of democracy via a free press, even though journalists have the highest mortality rates.  It also describes those who barely make it to three meals a day, unaware of their true plight.

If I remember it right, you said that words have a power of their own.  I know that some shamans/healers use the Sator square to invoke protection and cures.  I don't really know how that works, or if it is just some sort of placebo effect; or if it is the shaman/healer's ET guide who does the real work while the healer gets the credit.

Thanks, Sleeper, for being patient in reading lengthy posts like this one.  Next time I post, I'll keep it short.  Give my regards to Milty, somehow, I think he is Arepo...  hmm???

P.S: Many thanks to John Lear!  Just like so many others who eventually find their way here to this oasis, it was through the graces of the gallant suave ace pilot.  Hey, John, I really enjoyed reading your posts here, black humor or otherwise.  Also, from the interviews you granted, I like best that story about you racing past a P-51 fighter, flying on a Douglas B-26 medium bomber maintaining altitude at 75 feet, pushing the limits while staying in control (how's that for integrity?), and deflating some fighter pilot's ego.

**A:  Sator Square saying has Etruscan roots for what comes around goes around.  Karma, reincarnation, and dealings with the supernatural world.**

Q:  Hi Lou, what can you tell us about the Bigfoot that was hanging out in your secret garden?

**A:  Lazy, he didn't help me move a single rock.**

Q:  Why did you not get a him on video when you were filming the ruins?

**A:  They can be such hams in front of a camera; I didn't want to encourage him.**

Q:  Have you got any tips for seeing and interacting with them?

**A:  Don't interact but run. If you can. Like most ETs, they often paralyze the humans during encounters.**

Q:  From what I understand you could walk right past one and not even see it if they do not want to be seen.

A:  **No one is ever alone in the woods, day, or night.  For the most part they keep to themselves.**

Q:  Well I can imagine most aliens dislike humans because we're like primitive immature immoral savages compared to them.  But the ones that have a real big vendetta or grudge against us, what is the reason?

A:  **No rhyme or reason.  Some people simply enjoy hating others, so too some ET's. [Often due to past life stuff]**

Q:  You said that the psychotic Roman Emperors were that way because they were intimate/involved with strange aliens and some of it rubbed off on them.  Is this the reason some people in society are psychotic, like the really wacko serial killers?

A:  **Yes.**

Q:  … or was this something special to what was going on in Rome with those emperors?

A:  **Rome had an important and difficult job to do; it took all kinds of strange other earthly critters to get the job done.**

Q:  And you said some don't believe the renegades have left the former axis countries.  Are they still lurking there trying to twist and build them up again?  Will a country, like Germany, ever become a threat again?  They seem too small and 3 steps behind the USA in military regards to be a threat worldwide.  If anything, they currently seem to be one of the better "good" countries around.

**A:  Germany and Japan are powerful countries now.  Germany was less than 3rd world when Hitler came to power, due to WW1.  But no, they are not troublemakers as are some who were Allies during the war, Russia, USSR at the time.**

## Pg. 444— 2011-02-17

Q:  Hey Lou I just wanted you to comment on what I'm gonna post, pretty freaky if u ask me.

OK, so last Saturday I go to my girlfriend's house.  She has a younger sister and lives with both of her parents.  I notice her mom seems like something is on her mind and she asks us if we want to go to the cemetery to visit her dad who died a few years ago.  She rarely visits him but her 2 sisters and brother make it a monthly thing to do so.  However, there's a reason she's going to visit him [this time].  She tells me and my girlfriend while cooking, as she kept going up stairs and back checking on the food.  At the same time my girlfriend is getting ready her sister is fast asleep.  Well, when her mom went to check on the food, all the cupboards were open, EVERY single one of them and she thought her daughters opened them to mess with her, but they told her they did not.

When she told me this it gave me goose bumps and the chills!  That's not all; later that day her dad came home and while getting ready to leave for the cemetery, all of a sudden, we hear a loud bang!  It happened to be their whiteboard but was impossible for it too fall because of the way it was positioned against the wall!  There's just no way.  So that frightened us all.  So, me and my girlfriend sat in the hallway by her sisters' room which is about halfway open and all of a sudden it just slams shut!  OMG that really got to all of us, so we all began to pray.  That's pretty much it and nothing else has happened since thankfully.

Sorry if It sounded like I was rambling away (I'm using an iPod to type) but I just want your take on this.  Do you think it could have been my girlfriend's grandpa trying to communicate with them since they haven't visited for a while?

**A:  The dead don't really hang out at cemeteries; most have better things to do.  Visiting grave sites helps those who are alive and missing loved ones.  The dead don't miss the living.  Many of the dead have rejoined the living.**

**Hauntings and other paranormal shenanigans are caused by the living and sometimes by other lost and found entities without a life, for various reasons.**

Q: Lou, why does Neptune have so many moons?  Anything particularly mind exploding?  Like anything else isn't...LOL.

A:  Gas giant planets create moons.  Neptune has moons yet to be discovered.  Some of the moons have legs, metaphorically speaking, they come and go like ocean liners (large UFOs traveling through the solar system).


Q: Also, are there other planets in our solar system on Earth's level?  It would be funny to have another planet right in our vicinity that also plays the 'no life outside here' game.

A:  Not like Earth.


Q: Hello Sleeper, for the past few months I been a bit disconnected from all the ET activity I had been having for quite some time.  Sometimes you say Milton is away or not communicating with you, so I wonder if you sometimes get disconnected.  For me it's kind of scary.  I don't really like the idea of being left alone in this world like most normal people in it.  Not that I have the choice, but I miss the contact.

Do you too get your time off?  Have you ever missed Contact?

A:  I never get time off.  I've thought about complaining to the labor board, but they would think me a nut. I don' miss contact and have plenty of it even when Milton is not around.


Q: Would you have any idea why it stops?  Is it a sign that you're on the wrong path or possibly not doing what you should be doing?

A:  They show up when they need to.  Most of the time when they do show up, they don't leave a note, and certainly not a memory for most.

Q:  Once when I was young, I opened my big mouth one too many times and I was kind of dumped or not chosen for the job per say when it came to the paranormal.  That would suck if it happened again, that's why I'm asking.

**A:  If you expect to get anywhere in this world, never open your mouth concerning the paranormal.  Perhaps they are looking out for you.**

Q:  Lou, a question if you may.  Our human 'global' condition, is it heading the right way or downhill?

**A:  Like a piston, up and down; some go up some go down (pistons and economies).**

Q:  I mean resources, famine, quality of life etc.  Is there a chance we might abandon the monetary system in the near future?

**A:  No chance.**

Q:  I suspect everything is going to stay status quo, since it's a prison planet for most, not Disneyland.  But watching the global economy, monetary manipulations and all the dreadful structural aggression's, I'm getting sick, really sick.  People are really blind, and for a good reason, I guess.

**A:  The blind leading the blind.  It's always been that way down here, will always be that way down here.  The nations of the world have always been on the edge of disaster, much of it is written in the history books.  Nation against nation, famine, natural disasters.  Nothing has changed other than now we have the Internet and people are more aware of things.  But blind leaders will always find plenty of blind followers.**

Q:  I had a really strange UFO related dream a few days ago, all I can recall by now are just blurred images of crafts dancing in the sky and an important message or some other thing I needed to get.  Really hoped it might be Milty or some other cool entities not just a dream/imagination.

A:  **Milty has been away for some time now, not even a postcard or a fax!
I'm loving it.  He does text, but from where I don't know.**

## Pg. 445— 2011-02-19

Q:  Hey Lou what's up with all this recent UFO activity in Jerusalem?

A:  **There is a disturbance in the Middle East force.**

Q:  I also watched the "Mona Lisa" and the abandoned ship from the "Apollo
20" mission; my guess is that the fly over video showing the abandoned craft is
legit and the video showing the female humanoid is fake.  What do you think?
www.revver.com/video/797241/apollo-20-ebe-mona-lisa-16-mm-film/
www.revver.com/video/642275/alien-spaceship-on-the-moon-flyover-before-
landing-apollo-20/ Also who were they?  Anunnaki maybe?  Thanks a lot Lou!!!

A:  **Maybe.**

Q:  Who are the troublemakers other than Russia...LOL.  France, Canada, UK?  I
could see my country being heavily infiltrated by renegades.  Canada seems to
fall hook line and sinker for the other side of burning issues.  Iraq war, global
warming etc. we seem to follow the mantra the road to hell is paved with good
intentions...LOL.

A:  **The troublemakers are those trying to change the world and not
themselves.**

Q:  Lou said: *"A toothpick has a lot more room in it than most people think.  Put
a toothpick under a microscope and there is an infinite universe in it."* What do
you mean?  In a sense, isn't everything infinity since infinity goes both directions
infinitely?

A:  **There are more than both directions, and some things are finite.**

Q:  Lou said: *"ET technology will allow humans to venture further into the solar system, but only to certain parts of the solar system."*  Concerning what we know about this small solar system, how much would you say, percentage wise, don't we know concerning the land masses it contains etc.?

**A:  We know about ten percent or less.**


Q:  On a rough estimate, how much info haven't you revealed simply because you don't have the time or because it's to damaging/mind-boggling to the mind?

**A:  Most all the info remains hidden.**


Q:  Lou said: *"Once we move up the ladder of existence our freedom to move about the galaxies and other dimensions increases exponentially."*  Once we reach this point, are we able to go to any galaxy or dimension at will?

**A:  Yes and no.**


Q:  How about other universes and the other places outside our tiny universe in this small big picture?

**A:  There is simply too much stuff even for infinite existence.  How can that be?  It be!**


Q:  Today, the general view of science on dinosaurs in movies like Jurassic park, are they anywhere close to being correct?  And did they really die out 65 million years ago?  Wish they were still alive – what a sight that would be!

**A:  Dinosaurs of every kind unimaginable exist all over the galaxy and even in some parts of this solar system.**


Q:  Lou said: *"Star clusters are real cool playgrounds where higher beings mingle."*  Are they in physical form or a whole entirely different costume?

**A: Many costumes.**

Q: Have you been there, or do you know what it's like?

**A: Yes.**

## Pg. 446— 2011-02-20

Q: Lou, about the Varginha incident in Brazil, what happened there?  I mean, I know the whole story that went around, beings were seen by people, were captured, etc.  But what really happened?  How did they get there?  Where did they go, and why?

**A: Humans can't capture "real" extraterrestrials.**

Q: Lou said: *"Milty has been away for some time now, not even a postcard or a fax!  I'm loving it.  He does text, but from where I don't know."*  John Lear said: "Milton (Spot) has been over at my house for about 2 months now.  What is he doing?  He's 'thinking about it'.  What is he thinking about?

Well when he showed up, he asked me if I wanted to see Saturn and be able to remember it.  I said, Sure, of course!  So, he says, "Well let me think about it and by the way I need some Yoo-hoo.  Lots of it."  So, you can imagine I was pretty excited about going to Saturn and being able to remember it so I started packing in the Yoohoo's.  The problem is that this has been going on for two months now and every time I ask him about the trip to Saturn he says, "I'm thinking about it."

So now I'm not sure whether or not Spot is on the level.  He asked me to take him down to the Crazy Horse II, total nude place and he liked it so much we are going down there almost every night.  Well let me tell you Lou, that place ain't CHEAP.  But it's all about getting a ride to Saturn and being able to remember it.

Lou, maybe you could call him and tell him he is about to wear out his welcome and get him off the pot.  But gently like "Get off the pot, Spot", in case he is almost ready to take me.  Know what I mean?

**A:  I don't know John, two months, wow, and at the Crazy Horse.  Never been there.  In some places in the galaxy and a few states here in the US, you two might be considered married.  Saturn?  I don't think so.  Have you picked out silverware yet?**

Q:  You have told us that people we run into in this life are most likely people we have run into in past lives.  Now the people on this board, this is not your typical watering hole.  So, I'd say it more than likely that a few of us here have known each other in past lives.  But where it gets interesting is If I had to guess I'd say Milton has the ability to make a person interested or not in this board.  As in helping people get what you say or not.

Now, normally we all have guides and come from different factions but, in this case, we all seem to listen and understand what we can, even if it's totally different from what we each perceive and we get along.  I find that perplexing.

So, my Question is: does Milton have a screening process for people who will be accepted, to accept this info?

**A:  No screening, only screaming on the hairpin turns, where many get flung off. Happens a lot. Tolerance levels and all that.**

Q:  Does Milton know us from past lives?

**A:  Yes.**

Q:  Do you know some of us from past lives?

**A:  Some people sound familiar.**

Q:  John Lear: Lou said: *"When the ET's decide to make a few changes they rotate the earth on its axis, and it spins between one and one hundred eighty degrees to its former axis.  It gets really windy on some places of the earth when this happens."* [nnnn]: That'd be a real turn of events.

**John Lear** said: "When Lou checks in we will find out whether or not I was 'just kidding'.

**A: Must be some truth to it, Missouri turns into the arctic a few months every year.  This year was a doozy!**

Q:  I just saw this video in a thread on ATS.  Very intriguing, they said there is a fight running over there.

"Alien activity on ISS base" [video unavailable] what do you think?

**A: Not much of a fight, ISS is still up there.**

Q:  Hello Lou, What's the deal with Multi Vitamin pills?  Are they worth taking, especially if you don't eat meat?  Sorry, I know you're not a nutritionist; next thing I'll be asking you how to fix my plumbing or defrag my hard drive etc., but actually I think this question might just be on the outer edge of the solar system of questions that you can deal with...Let me know if I'm wrong.

**A: Multi Vitamins and many other legal drugs in Western countries are a waste of money and can create other problems.  But for those whose diets are bad, vitamins can be helpful.  Some people swear by them, some swear at them.**

## Pg. 447— 2011-02-21

Q:  No doubt, but if you mean to point out that "Jesus" may have drawn assertion that he was "god" -that's an interesting point of specific clarity I was looking for. It reflects a who's who in both MAN & ET elitist agenda.

**A: There was no Jesus person with 12 disciples and a John...the Baptist. There were many people named Jesus back in Jesus' time.  Heck there is a billion dudes named Jesus in the city of Lost Angels.  The name is common now and way back then too.  All religions are false, regardless if their prophets were real humans or fictional.**

Q:  Now two random run-of-the-mill questions for Lou.  How are you today?  Do you have anything fun planned this week?

A:  **I'm fine thank you!  The weather is sunny, that's fun.**


Q:  **John Lear** said: "No.  He wants to go to Tiffany's in New York.  I told him there was a branch store here in Vegas and he informed me that he was 'high maintenance' and he didn't go to 'branch' stores.  I am not of his 'persuasion' but I'll do just about anything for a trip to Saturn and be able to remember.  Just about.

A:  **Milton, high maintenance?  You have no idea John...LOL and you want to go to Saturn with him...and remember.  You have any idea the cost!  Take him to Tiffany's, your wallet with thank you.**


Q:  Hi Lou, you said the places in our dreams are very real.  I have had a few very vivid and at the time very real feeling dreams; one where I was working in a mine under the direction of strange creatures and one where I was sent to infiltrate this group of really evil entities and they found me out and attacked me and chased me ...LOL it wasn't a terribly pleasant dream.

If these places and things are very real, do I exist in some parallel life in some far away strange place?  And what does this mean?

A:  **Experiencing things don't mean you actually jumped out of a plane without a parachute.  When we watch a movie or go to Disney World or some such place, we "get" the experience, feel of things long past or perhaps future event. It means souls live in a dynamic reality/universe.**


Q:  Also, after I asked to go on one of Milton's rides and you said Milton was done for the moment, but others would be taking people.  I had a strange dream where I was being chased by something frightening and then this woman approached me and said "enough of the scary stuff" and she flagged down this light in the sky which was this pink haze of an entity that appeared in front of us and I could feel this "goodness" and warmth of an aura just radiating from it and

I got to ask it three questions, which I didn't at the time feel like I had much control over. They were:

1. Am I a good person?

2. Did I used to be an Anunnaki (...LOL I didn't have control of that question)

3. When is my time on earth done?

It answered:

1. Yes, you are (it paused for one second before it said that ...LOL)

2. Doesn't matter

3. Laughed and said I can't tell you that.

Do you think any of this is real or is my dreams just strange?

**A: Sounds like strange dreams to me. And as I've said often, dreams are real and strange places.**


Q: **John Lear** said: [in response to a Jesus question answered many times] "Lou, try speaking in Italian. Maybe his first language wasn't English"

**A: You got it John, here's a warmup. [YT video deleted]**

## Pg. 448— 2011-02-23

Q: Lou, I was wondering, after death, do we experience the vibes we created in a linear way or is it all put in a blender? Is all the happiness and unhappiness one creates in life stirred into a glass and given to us to be swallowed whole, or is it all separated?

**A: Everything is specific to the dot, except for Milton's answers. He prefers to blend his Yoohoo's with bits of other stuff mixed in.**


Q: The reason I ask is this; supposing I've spent all my life asleep (spiritually speaking) or worse, upsetting people a lot of the time and occasionally making some happy, almost through random chance. Will I thus far have mostly very unpleasant sensations awaiting me?  But if I have some sort of epiphany, hit the brakes and then spend what time I have left creating as many positive vibes as I can, everything I've ever done mixed into a glass might just about be edible, without severe stomach cramps.  On the other hand, if I have to sit through an interactive movie of all I've done it would just be more a case of having to eat my brussels sprouts up, no putting my dinner into a blender allowed, no dumping half of it my bib or putting other bits on someone else's plate.

I rather fear you're going to tell me it's the second.

**A:  It all boils down to the "why".  Why do we do what we do.**

**• Do we do things because that's who we are?**

**• Do we love helping others, being cheerful, enjoy the joy others experience rather than despise them?**

**• Do we do things because we fear for our own welfare?**

**• Would you steal if you knew you would never get caught?**

**• Would you harm someone if you knew you never would be harmed in return?**

**All of us have met both types of people and all of us know which types we prefer to be around.  The higher ups know which people they want at their family picnics too.  The vast majority of people don't buy into this claptrap. If they did, the world would be Utopia.  That ain't ever going to happen.**

Q:  Lou, John told me on his forum that the good guys were the ones who destroyed the planet that is now the asteroid belt.  Are these ETs the same?  (The ones that did the towing job)

**A:  Not the same.  And good is relative to the situation, not as in relationship.**

Q:  Also, did these two events happen – one because of the other?

**A:  No.**

Q:  Hi there Lou and Milton!  Thank you for the great work and for everything you have done!  What can you and Milton say about people, who work in structures like: CIA, MI6 and other secret agencies?  How spying & stealing info for their country influences them individually?  Are secret agents from third and second world countries working for some renegades' agenda?

**A:  Yes. This is a complex prison planet for most, school planet for some, hell for many and a Paradise for a few.  Like gears in machinery, renegades and human counterparts churn and grind at human souls, separating wheat from chaff kind of thing.  A lot of things are happening without the herd ever knowing, not an easy lullaby.**

Q:  Hi Lou!  I know the universe has ALWAYS existed, but was there ever a point-in-time when there was absolutely nothing in it?

**A:  Never.**

Q:  Lou said: *"We exist in a soup of entities, and at these lower levels, both good and bad things swim around us all the time.  It's a blessing that most can't see such creatures."*

Do the entities on Uranus and other planets in our solar system see these things?

**A:  Some and if they choose, but only lower areas have the flees and other blood/soul sucking pests.**

Q:  Lou said: *"The big picture and there are many big pictures, are all filled with spectacular and delightful stuff.  So much more than people could ever hope to absorb in forever land.  Most souls will eventually enter those domains."*

The domains you speak of are places such as Uranus and Saturn?  No?

**A:  And beyond and places like Earth too, for those with eyes open.**

Q:  Is life possible on starless planets, solar systems, galaxies?

**A:  Various forms of unique, exotic, and intelligent life exists everywhere.**

Q:  Lou said: *"Because time is an illusion, those who have died and went to the other side could have lived many lives on other places and then returned to the in-between place and still be a guide."*  Is there any way possible for you to put in words how time works, or shall I say doesn't work the way we think?  And so, let's say the amount of time it takes me when I drop a pen on the floor.  Someone, somewhere else in this universe or elsewhere could have already lived an entire lifetime or more in that span of one second on earth?

**A:  Building blocks, each have their own time, and can be stacked any which way by higher beings.**

Q:  If the future is both predetermined and not written in stone, then how does time travel work?

**A:  Time travel can be manipulated and facilitated by ET.  Humans are sometimes shown future events and or taken for a ride to past events.**

Q:  Can you create a future with what you want to happen?

**A:  No, but it can be created for you.**

Q:  And what about alternate realities?  Thank you!

**A:  No shortage of alternate realities, we even visit a few in dreamland.**

Q:  Lou said: *"There was no Jesus person with 12 disciples and a John...the Baptist."*

Understood.  Course strict, historical reference accounting isn't the point of interest.  Which boils down to questioning whether Milton is saying "karma" is not one's reactionary-cumulative baggage, by reflection of manufactured illusion of good & evil?

Lou said: *"Good and evil are illusions and nothing more than programs running on this computer, we call earth."*

Beyond that, Milton's reference line regarding "Jesus" matches up with other ET accounting, least in the strict language of your replies.  Your first being "god" never walked the earth – which is clearly the truth of it given we're all fractal projection of "god" or what is the Intelligent Cosmos.  To that "Jesus of Nazareth" or the "King of Kings" went by the name of Jehoshua and didn't solicit or formalize followers or "Disciples."

**A:  No fractals/illusions of such beings set foot on this planet either.**

Q:  Does Milton agree that 'in forgiveness lies the stoppage of the wheel-of-action, or what you call karmic-retribution'?

**A:  It stops the accumulation, and gives respite to the forgiver, for the duration of forgiveness during this life.  Milton loses many on these kinds of sharp turns.  You do the crime you "will" do the time.  Forgiveness, yes, pardon no.**

**Good and evil is illusion but acting out on one or the other is the real deal.  A sting operation is a setup to catch those with "intent", to see what one is made of and get it on film.  Once on film the perpetrator is shown his/her deeds/weaknesses.  No debate, no judgment, only proof.**

**Karma is the only real constant in the universe.  "Sweetened" cool aid, not served on this site.**

Q:  Hi Lou, I have been doing some research today and have a question.  If you build up a lot of karmic debt before you die, does this affect how soon you must reincarnate back to earth to pay it off so to speak?

**A:  Depends on the crime: mass murderer or shoplifting, and level of hate simmering in the soul.**

# Pg. 449— 2011-02-24

Q:  What is this "disturbance in the force", hehe that is going on in the Middle East and parts of Africa?  Old dictatorships are falling, mass protests are happening and the people in their eyes are gaining their freedom.

**A:  Obviously, the Internet has opened up a world of "easy living" that many experience to those who are denied such luxuries as freedoms.  Those living the "good life of freedom" in places like Europe and the Americas, the free people, are restless too.**

**The whole world is a restless tormented place, where people are seldom happy with their lot in life.  The grass is always greener on the other side kind of thing.  Here in America we have democracy out the ears, and yet many, if they could, would change that.**

Q:  Mind you, the Russians who overthrew the monarchy in the Russian revolution probably thought the same thing and that led them down the communist Stalin/Soviet era where things were just as horrible.

**A:  Things were not just as horrible; they became more so after the Bolsheviks destroyed all forms of freedom and made everyone equal.  Cattle are equal, and the Soviet/Russian people were treated less than cattle.  Much of that horrific history has been whitewashed, but for those interested they can find info on that horrific era.**

Q:  ET must be pulling the strings here, what is the agenda?

**A:  ET allows many things to unfold, like petals on a flower.  Some for the good, some for the bad.**

**Like the Tower of Babel, where the people of the Earth were determined to equate and hobnob with the gods.  The build up to 2012 through the Internet, movies, and books, has unleashed similar desires.**

**What is in store for this "new" Tower of Babel?  Like in Wisconsin, Milton has gone into hiding.**

Q:  Hi, Lou said: *"The big picture and there are many big pictures, are all filled with spectacular and delightful stuff.  So much more than people could ever hope to absorb in forever land.  Most souls will eventually enter those domains."*

Now, this at least made me happy, though I do feel it's ALL, eventually.  With infinities within/without, what would happen if you turned an atom or even a planet inside out, would there be an infinite universe on the reverse side?  Could we be in such a place?

A:  **Milton's cousin Vinny, pig lizard Gorgnak once was turned inside out, it wasn't pretty.**

**Galaxy Quest – Funny Part Gorgnak**:
https://www.youtube.com/watch?time_continue=2&v=eVEncwqBcko


Q:  They grow cars on the vine, so to speak.  Are crafts grown on the vine as well?  Mercedes-Benz BIOME Concept – could cars be grown in a lab?
Www.gizmag.com/mercedes-benz-biome-concept/17096/

A:  **I don't know about growing them on vines, Milty built his ship in his garage when he was a kid a billion years ago.**


Q:  Lou said: *"No screening, only screaming on the hairpin turns, where many get flung off."*

Does Milton like to use accents when he speaks English, by any chance?

A:  **Yes, he likes to imitate Groucho Marx a lot.  The cigar smoke gets him hacking though and ruins it.  I've told him not to light the cigar, but does he listen?**


Q:  I know what you mean though.  When the time comes, and you have the chance to know.  Well I can't imagine how big the size of a person's balls have to be to not fly off on a sharp turn.  It's funny but I know full well, I beg not to have ever seen an ET and know 100% if it ever happened while I was awake in a normal 3D state. But still I hope it happens someday. It's nice when you see them in an altered state though. You get the beast of both worlds. I think, or maybe I was just dreaming.... See what I mean Wooo!

Sleeper, do people willingly opt to see an ET and know when they get the option?

**A:  ET's prefer to be unpredictable.**


Q:  Just as info, or programming, or are we an ongoing project of his?  "Why", is what I'm getting at, if I may?  [Nnnn] crosses his fingers and hopes Sleeper is in one of his worm can opening moods.

**A:  Yes, on the ongoing project, BTW, how's the project coming along?  No one gets to know what their project is other than it is a can of worms, or sometimes seems that way?**


Q:  Just as you once remarked (if memory serves) that taking drugs is cheating. Couldn't the same be said of NDE's and the information you've given us in your books and especially in forums?

**A:  Doing drugs will give glimpses of things, BUT NOT things that will move one up the ladder of existence.  Moving up is not on everyone's' agenda. Info received via NDE or from anywhere else that helps turn a soul around doesn't happen by accident.**


Q:  We've been given some of the answers before the exam has finished, as it were.  Lou, there is no doubt that had I not read about NDE's and read your stuff the wakeup call would have taken a lot longer.  I like to think my conscience would have eventually got there on its own, but I'm very ashamed to say that civilizations might have risen and fallen in the meantime.  I've always believed that if you want to live in a good universe you have to create a good universe.  Be the change you want to see and all that.  But faced with a million different possibilities at every turn, I almost never pick the optimum one because I've been cautiously checking what the play is.  Don't worry, I'm sending myself right back and I'm already shaking my head at myself in despair.  Would I want a picnic with myself?  Probably not, to be honest.

**A:  With such "awakened" attitude I wouldn't pass up any invitations to a picnic.  After all, the gods make the rules and send invitation to whomever they want.**


Q:  Well, looks like I am shit out of luck.  If 'drugs' are cheating.  Not hard drugs, but I love to drink vodka and beer, I have a good time.  Guess I will have to pay the consequences and that my soul is troubled, as Lou says.

Lou, does this make me an evil person?  Can you ask Milton if I am an evil person because he knows me from a past life?

**A:  Drinking a little vodka and beer now and then doesn't make one evil.  Evil people don't buy into what this site spews.  There are some evil people hanging around this site, however.  Few people know they are evil or have evil tendencies, that's why they are on Earth, to sniff out these hidden tendencies and maybe root them out when they do.**


Q:  Lou thanks for the response; no mass murder, no hate simmering, but I am sure my list is long and varied.

**A:  Those people not adding to the "long and varied" are way ahead of the pack.**


Q:  **John Lear** said: No, he's not in hiding.  We're in New York picking out a ring.  He told me today he wants an Armani suit.  I said, "Spot, do you have any idea how ridiculous you would look in an Armani suit?  A blob with a suit on is still a blob."  "Well Lou has one", he came back.  "No Spot, Lou doesn't have an Armani suit.  And neither do I."

Anyway, we went down to Coney Island.  Spot wanted a ride on the roller coaster to see what life was like as a human here on earth.  We went to 'ground zero' yesterday and he looks in this gigantic hole and says, "That's less than kids' stuff." Go figure.

A:  **Milton promised me an Armani suit and some bling-bling years ago, but the dude has no money.  I was wondering how he was going to pull it off.  So, what kind of ring did you get him, John?  One of those big gold ones with a huge diamond in the middle?**

## Pg. 450— 2011-02-25

Q:  Lou said: *"No fractals/illusions of such beings set foot on this planet either. Zip, nada!"*

That's an interesting and descriptive response Lou, in and of itself.  Ultimately: considering polar opposite ET conveyance necessarily suggests ET is either lying, misinformed, malinformed, or of a skewed perspective to variable reason.

A:  **Milton is NOT misinformed, malinformed or in possession of a skewed perspective to a variable reason.  The fact is most humans can't handle the truth – so the truth remains hidden from them.  No fancy words going to change that.**


Q:  When Milton describes 'karma as being the only real constant in the universe', is he saying MAN, and or ET is inextricably non-cooperative?

A:  **He is saying man is lazy when it comes to integrity and virtue.**


Q:  Yeah, when I was typing that I was thinking it was probably worse during the Stalin years than any other for Russia.  I understand Karma and I know this isn't a happy ending planet.  But why did, whoever was pulling the strings(ET) let/want/allow Russia to devolve into that living hell of communism –  they just overthrew the monarchy and got their "freedom", you would think they would have got some small reprieve.

A:  **They received what was coming to them, no more, no less.  So did their children and children's' children, etc.**

Q:  It's like a German Jew who fought in the war for Germany in WW1, survives that horrific trench warfare and then has to suffer the holocaust during the WW2 years.  It's so extreme; why would anybody ever deserve to experience such hell.

**A:  From the perspective of those experiencing such hell's, with no memory of why, there is no good reasons.  But say I rape, murder and pillage for the fun of it in one lifetime, what should my punishment be? Reward in my next incarnation?**

Q:  What ET factions controls/influences Russia?

**A:  Bolsheviks, Marxists, Communists spewing Renegades.**

Q:  They fought Germany on the eastern front in WW2 in which can only be described as the bloodiest most ferocious war of atrocities in known human history.  Yet the Germans were the poster children of the renegades and the good guy allies were on Milton's side.  Where does that leave Russia in the big picture?  They probably won the war for the allies against the Germans, yet the soviets, especially Stalin were extremely evil.

**A:  The Soviets were with Hitler originally, but like gangsters fought over territory and the division of European spoils.  Socialist Hitler wanted all the spoils and so did the Communist Soviets. Greed divided them and weekend both. Is why the Allies won.**

Q:  I'm back with a random question that's been bugging me for months; I'd appreciate your thoughts on it (and anyone's for that matter).  My daughter used to talk about "things" that would come at night, she told me a lot of stories about where they went and what happened.  The re-occurring thing was that they reminded her of Boohbah's (kids TV program), she said they were blue; she's also had a green one and a lady with blonde hair.

Is there a type of ET that fits the description of a boohbah?  If so, why do they upset her so much?

**A:  Every type unimaginable exists.  ET's move faster than hummingbirds and humans don't, that creates confusion and fear, for most.**

Q:  Just in case you have no idea what a Boobah is here is a video [YT deleted video my guess of equal] https://www.youtube.com/watch?v=NQ-nif4rXGs they come on screen at about 2 minutes in.

**A:  Wow, maybe now I can get Milton to sit still while drinking his Yoohoo's in front of the television.**

Q:  Lou, our personalities do not stay with us, right?

**A:  We retain aspects of personality.**

Q:  We come back with a clean slate and try to learn again?

**A:  No try, only do.**

Q:  Does our soul entity begin to develop a certain pattern after many returns to 3D?

**A:  We come off the rack, brought into existence, with a personality good enough to write home about.  Some will regain it over the barrel of time, intact would be preferable.  Only then does the real show begin.**

Q:  Lou said: *"What are atoms?  They are made up of bits and pieces of freaky energy thingies.  What are freaky energy thingies?  Nothing at all.  Illusions for 3D land."*

Can you explain that contradiction?

**A:  Energy is but an illusion on lower platforms of existence.  Energy is a tool for learning, a sandbox to play in.  Higher ups don't use or need energy of any kind, as we humans understand energy, in their everyday lives.  They don't even have "everyday lives".**

Q:  Or are we seeing more than just 3D lands?  There is certainly some strange looking stuff when looking at Hubbell space shots.  Are we seeing more than just our 3D illusionary "reality"?

Lou said: *"We see things that we don't understand in 3D land, above and below 3 dimensions is more skewed."*

What do you mean?  How about galaxies and such that look like gigantic eyes or like gods?

**A:  Gods don't come down to sandbox level, they hire mercenaries.  What we see in the night skies is a whole lot of magic and endless seas of galaxies, suns, and planets with similar life forms as ours, some more bizarre, some less.  There are numerous kinds of so-called intelligent life going on in every crevice in this universe of which 99.99999...% humans will never see or comprehend while in their birthday suits.**

Q:  Lou said: *"Yes, we can reach Milton's level and higher."*

Is there a ceiling for us?

**A:  You mean like a glass ceiling?  Yes, for some types of souls.**

Q:  Lou said: *"Souls are not scaled.  Something else is at work."*

No rank of souls and the infinite variations and infinite things beyond souls? What's at work?

**A:  Virtue for starters.  Then something unexplainable to the un-virtuous.**

Q:  Lou said: "*Nevertheless, most of the good stuff is on levels above us, and the good stuff is in your face and no one can ignore it like they do down here.*"

Good stuff down here like enjoying a stroll through a park or through our beautiful scenery such as the vast breathtaking view of the Grand Canyon and also all the beautiful creatures we have here.  How does it compare to "above us"?  Utopia or beyond?  Those places on a miraculous dose of steroids compared?

**A:  All the beauty and awesome things we have down here only compare to a baby rattle a few notches up on Utopia planets.  Beyond Utopia there is no ceiling and wonder and awe can't touch what is going on.**

Q:  Lou said: "*As long as we have a body, we are not alive.  To really live is to be free from matter.*"

What do you mean?  Are you talking about soul form and other things in non-matter existences?

**A:  Even a matter-less soul can weigh on us.**

Q:  The rest you can get at <u>www.lawofone.info</u>, but this isn't a pissing contest.  And it surprises me that no one has drawn specific questioning of Milton's disposition.  If so, I would like to hear more.

Channeled information?  So, Ra does know Ishtar.

**John Lear**: You are truly a great man!!  I love your responses to Mr.  [nnnn], they are classic and genuine of course as I would like an answer to **ALL** the questions you asked him.  LOL!!!

Lou, John, and everyone on the board, I hope you are all doing well these days, I know I am!!  Today, after I left a meeting with my customer, I called up my mother just to say hello and after we talked for a few minutes she asked why I called her.  Hehe, of course she figured I was in some kind of trouble or something, like all mothers say to their sons I think when they call outa the blue.

I told her that I just wanted to say, 'hi and that I love you'!  It made her day, according to her words...and it made my day as well.

Hope you all on the board doing just as great today as well!!  Take care and remember to look up at the stars, it always makes me happy...and to tell your loved ones that you love them!!

**A:  Some people chase after their tails looking for wisdom and an invitation to Mensa, when the real path to Nirvana is the simple things in life most overlook, like "it made her day".  And yours too.**

## Pg. 451 — 2011-02-27

Q:  Hi Lou, You said we are never alone in the "woods" I live on 10 acres of forested area that backs onto 100's of acres of the same when I take my dogs for walks I always feel like I'm being watched...LOL, what sort of paranormal entities live in the woods?

**A:  All kinds of entities exist in the woods and the concrete jungles too. Humans can't escape from them. Good thing most are harmless.**

Q:  And why don't they let me see them since I'm the only one out there and I'm probably willing...LOL?

**A:  Apparently you are off limits, that's a good thing.  But when and if they do stop and chat, those allowed to approach you, they mostly hit you with the Neuralyzer thingy.  Smile for the camera.**

## Pg. 452 — 2011-03-01

Q:  Hello Sleeper!  Did the Sun spit out any planets with this recent Solar Flare? Www.space.com/10960-sun-whips-massive-flare.html

**A:  I didn't see any mention of such phenomena in my morning newspaper.**

Q:  Lou said: *"Some people chase after their tails looking for wisdom and an invitation to Mensa, when the real path to Nirvana is the simple things in life most of us overlook, like "it made her day"*.

Sheesh, you can say that again!  The trouble is, we think we have time, and so habitually indulge the discursive mind, the meaning-making mind, running around in circles, listening first to this guy, then to that guy, trying to figure it all out, and meanwhile missing what it's really all about in the first place.

Everyone wants to love and be loved – it's really pretty simple – but our ideas, beliefs, and arrogant convictions keep us tripping over our own shoe laces, while we waste our lives attempting to make the world conform to the way we imagine it should be.

I put no faith in the conscious – it's a house of tricks.  Sure, there's a place for the intellect, as long as we realize that nothing that we can conceptualize is real, and in fact, the assumption that we are or someday will be "knower's" is one of the biggest cons going.

Plain truth is, at this level, we don't know jack.  I work in a residential treatment center for advanced Alzheimer patients, and at one time, each resident had an active mind filled with all the lovely ideas about themselves and the world and God and so forth, but each day I watch as everything they thought they knew slips away, inexorably.  Each patient is a mirror and a teaching, but who wants to even take a good hard look, much less go on and do the work it takes to discover what truly remains when all the distracting crap that we believe to be "our life" drops away?

A:  **That "distracting crap" is what makes life worth living for those with blinders on.**
**Life is a conveyor belt; those entering don't see what is going on with those exiting.  Nursing homes filled with Alzheimer patients, the old, the injured, condemned to live final years stripped of dignity, comfort, sanity, and freedom.  It all happens so fast and one day when we least expect it the trap door slams shut, test over, put down the pencils.**

Q:  Hi Lou, haven't read it but there was a strange novel in the 19ᵗʰ century
called: Vril The Power of The Coming Race.  It was about a subterranean race
deep inside the earth and this substance called Vril and how this group of beings,
while living in Utopia like conditions, was a danger to earth.  Apparently, many
took it for a real account of information including Hitler and the Nazi's and the
supposed "Vril Society" was based off this novel.  They believed this was their
"Aryan" group of beings.  Was this the subterranean group that allied itself with
Hitler's Nazi's during WW2?

**A:  They were and are in the game under other guises (reptilian).**


Q:  And are you able to shed any more light or drips on what happened exactly to
Hitler?  I read even though Stalin had possession of Hitlers "remains" when he
took control of Berlin, he believed until his own death that Hitler was still alive.

**A:  No drips other than he was removed from Germany alive.**


Q:  Lou, I promise this is my last post re; animals.  Contrary to what I always
believed, your hints that they are not sentient but effectively no different to
"toasters"  has got me dreaming of sausages, and more importantly, hopeful that
it really is the case that all the terrible things that happen to animals is a kind of
illusion.  I think what you're saying is plausible, because animals are innocent
and therefore in my book, don't deserve to suffer at all.  Still, I'm hedging my
bets and going to remain a vegetarian, as I'm reasonably healthy and I think it
sets a good example to others.  Anyway, even if paradoxically, animals do not
actually suffer.  After all, most people vaguely believe animals suffer and eat
them anyway.  Given what you know, is it correct to say that ultimately it doesn't
matter how animals are treated in captivity, how they are killed and so on?

**A:  It does matter how we treat animals.  How we treat animals tells a whole
bunch about the soul doing the treating.  For one, no one knows who or what
is inside an animal at any given moment, past family members included.
Many human souls end up inside of animals. Voluntarily as a way to visit
with loved ones on Earth, but also as punishment.**

Q:  If the answer is that it matters, with whom does the responsibility rest to make sure they are well treated?  There are so many people in the equation: consumer, fast food chain, supplier to fast food chain, supplier to supplier, slaughterhouse, supplier of equipment to slaughterhouse, law makers who regulate slaughterhouses, voters who vote for their lawmakers, etc.  It seems to me everyone has their bit somewhere along the line and not pass the buck.

**A:  The buck stops with those on the frontline of the slaughter. Are they cruel or principled? Same is true with soldiers whose job is to kill.**


Q:  When it comes down to it, do people who live without hate, greed or envy stop to think about the process the bacon in their sandwich went through?

**A:  People that reach such level of virtue need not worry about it; they are removed from this blood, guts and hamburger with fries, planet.**


Q:  Probably just a worry of a man who has got his worries in the wrong order, but input appreciated.

**A:  Mother Nature treats animals like animals, and we all know how ugly, cruel, and vile existence in the wild is for animals, without humans being involved.**


Q:  Lou, where do fairy tales come from; three little pigs, red riding hood?  I think you mentioned once that she ate the wolf, not the wolf ate the grandma.

**A:  Fairy tales come from politicians, scientists, and religious leaders.  Red riding hood ate the wolf?  If I said that, it was in jest, but a good twist to the story.**

Q:  According to an interview with a British correspondent years after the Great War, Hitler claimed a mysterious voice told him to leave a section of a crowded trench during a minor barrage.  Moments after he left the area, a shell fell on that spot.  Hitler saw this experience as a message that he was a uniquely illuminated individual who had a special task to fulfill.  This story did not, however, appear in Mein Kampf.  Any truth to that?

**A:  Actual physical "beings" told him/advised him concerning that and other dangers.  He was protected supernaturally and knew it.  Hitler was primed for the mission he accomplished.**

Q:  Lou said: *"That 'distracting crap' is what makes life worth living."*

To clarify, when I say "distracting crap", I'm referring to the cumulative clutter that blinds us from what life (love) is really all about – the greed and acquisitiveness, the envy, simmering hatreds, pettiness, allegiance to beliefs in twisted doctrines and religious bigotry, the fascination with power and privilege, the relentless efforts at self-confirmation – all that binds us to this dreamy rock.

**A:  I knew what you meant and for many that is what makes life worth living, lost to the true wonders of life.**


Q:  Hi Lou it's been a while.  I hope you and yours are well and that goes for everyone on the forum.  Well Lou, we lost the family dog.  He was a real friend and my son's best pal and they even slept together.  He died young.

The question is Lou; if we reach those high levels of integrity and get to a better place can we have the exact same dog back?  I/we miss our walks in the woods with him big time and his parting has broken my family and my heart real bad.  I don't mind saying that every time I look at his lovely face I just go to bits with grief.

Question is Lou, if we reach those high levels of integrity can we have the dog back; after all, if they create all those things out there in space surely, they can make us the same dog.  Now he was a beautiful piece of ET high tech and gave us more pleasure than most things in this life and I don't mind saying that we are really miffed with the high ups for snatching him away from us.  We are so utterly shattered at his departure.  Maybe you could have a word with Milton.

A:  **It's not the package, it's what's in the package; dog, cat, horse, human. Whatever or whoever was in the dog will always be part of the family.  The family exists forever.  Everyone has a huge family, and "other things", beings, on the other side, waiting, watching.**

## Pg. 453 — 2011-03-02

Q:  Hi Lou, down here in New Zealand we are still reeling from a major earthquake last week, in the fair city of Christchurch.  There was massive damage and loss of life, our country weeps.  The thing is the event was predicted by a "maverick" mathematician by the name of Ken Ring.  Ken believes that the gas giants, Jupiter, and Saturn effect the sun (their gravity causes sunspots) which in turn effects Earth (earthquakes) when they all line up.  He also believes that the moon is the major influence in our planets weather, which sort of makes sense to me.  I was hoping you might have some info about this, Cheers.

A:  **The moon is part of earth's dynamics.  The planets have little consequence on sun dynamics.**


Q:  Is Milton making Yoo-hoo Moonshine Sleeper?  Thanks,

A:  **He ain't had a lick of sense since.**


Q:  Lou said: *"The adventures of a Milty"*

That would make one awesomely kick ass book, and I would love to read it!  So, Sleeper, when's it coming out?

A:  **Part one is Milty making moonshine, communing with nature, animals, and a cranky wife.**


Q:  Hey Sleeper and All.  There were many times where I dissed or hurt people without knowing it – it was NOT my intent.  One thing this board has taught me is to think things through a lot more before acting to avoid those unintended consequences.  Are we liable for all our actions, even the unintended?

A: "The road to hell is paved with good intentions," as an old saying goes. I'd hate to think where "un-intentions" take us when good intentions take us straight to hell.

Every intention is scrutinized once we get to the other side. You will be the harshest judge of your actions.

Q: Sleeper, Space is infinite? Space is nothingness? Space allows us a place to sense/guesstimate dimensions, 3D planets, people, places, things. Is there only one space or are there other empty places where stuff happens? WTF am I asking...LOL!

A: Sounds like you are spaced out [nnnn]. There are infinite other "spaces" where stuff happens.

Q: This is too cute...made me smile all day: Baby Laughs hysterically Over Tearing Up Paper www.liveleak.com/view?I=661_1298894854

A: It don't get any better than a baby's laugh!

Q: Lou, on another subject, there's been a lot of talk lately about solar activity, and the possibility that a coronal mass ejection could take down the power grid for an extended period. Do you see something like that scenario materializing in the next few years?

A: Milton says yes, but he's been in the moonshine and going through a personal brain power grid failure himself.

## Pg. 454 — 2011-03-04

Q: In your books you mentioned the watch you got on the station close to the sun was 'biodegradable' in Earth atmosphere. Is this biodegradable property based on inter-dimensional vibrational changes?

A: Nothing fancy like that. I think Milton took it.

Q:  It seems as if the tools on the alien ship in your book (*In League*.) were able to communicate directly with the body and even with the soul.  Apart from direction given by the surgeons, do these tools also need directions given by the body and even permission from the soul of the person operated on in order to work?

A:  **There are things at play no one knows about except the freaky gadgets themselves.**

Q:  Is the community still exploring the alien ship and its contents?

A:  **Yes.**

Q:  Is Hyperion, Saturn's moon, a prison?

A:  **Hyperion has a prison or two on it like most rocks in the solar system.**

Q:  Hey Lou, you mentioned something about expeditions to the poles by some countries to dig up some E.T. stuff.  I wonder if there has been, or there will be, a situation like that in John Carpenter's movie "The Thing"?  Thanks as always.

A:  **Most definitely, but unlike in Hollywood movies, the "Alien Things" are impervious to human attempts to kill or subdue.  Such things serve as mechanisms limiting what mankind can latch on to and make their own. Every scrap, morsel comes with a cost factor.**

Q:  You have said many of the characters in the bible; Enoch, Adam and eve, Moses etc. are codes and metaphors and that the codes are too long and complex to explain.  Who is the real information from these stories intended for; since I assume its "coded" so us human folk can't piece the real story together?

A:  **Crop circles and other markings are message for certain "other" beings. This planet has many road signs appropriate to those able to understand them, and them only.  A sign language of sorts.**

Q:  And is the book of Enoch or the character Enoch a renegade code, since it's a forgotten book of the bible?  Thanks.

**A:  The book of Enoch is not lost; was always available to some.  There are many books that have been taken off planet or hidden away from humans and are really lost.**

## Pg. 455 — 2011-03-05

Q:  **John Lear**; Great Enoch question [nnnn].  I would have asked it myself, but Lou is still a little ticked that I took Spot to New York without him.  He has nothing to worry about though.  Spot left me taking with him the Armani suit I bought him and the ring I bought at Tiffany's (cost me $99 plus tax).

I took him to eat a genuine hot dog on Broadway; took him on the ferry boat to the Statue of Liberty; took him to Central Park; took him for lunch at the top of the World Trade Center (he had to take us back in time for that one) took him to Greenwich village and then he flat disappears leaving me with his unused airline ticket back to Vegas.  Said he'd be in the vicinity of Saturn doing some kind of business.  That little alien weasel.

**A:  Doing some kind of business in the vicinity of Saturn my arse, Milton got him one of "these" and is doing his business with his Armani and hundred dollar watch on the third rock.**

**Long as I Got One Of These, by Harriette McClure:**
https://www.youtube.com/watch?v=zMOSCvnR08Q


Q:  I've been following and just think everyone is asking such good questions, and the answers, even while I suspect they're just a glimpse of things, I'm surprised this isn't the top-rated site online.  It's so obvious what's being discussed are the most important things I can imagine, aside from just day by day kindness and unraveling whatever is blocking our kindness.

Lou, I have a question that is bugging me about experiences.  If for example, you've seen a craft several times in a week, and whether or not I see them, I can still pick up whatever energy they employ.  I don't know if its antigravity or what really.  But, after seeing the crafts, I was bringing groceries into the house just after it was dark and there were two shadows, one was a very tall under the tree branch – saw a whole outline, but the other was identical to the ruddy pink colored "grey" I saw, a solid shadow, same height, build, very thin almost twig like.  But it's the way he moved.

The movements they make are surreal, long striding, fluid, hard to describe before they disappear, movements we could never duplicate.  I often thought this would be from DUMBS or underground cloning programs with the black ops, but I can't see how they get those movements?  Is this an entity manifesting or a body suit?

**A:  It's a projection of whatever they allow you to see. When they enter your space atoms and quarks discombobulate.**

Q:  When a person sees crafts, and possibly more, i.e., something moving like the ET they saw in their garden, and stays up as late as possibly not giving permissions for nighttime activity or visits, does it matter?

**A:  Matters not.**

Q:  Does it matter if one puts off sleep until they're forced to bed, or is this futile and they should just go to sleep anyway, because they can be accessed no matter what?

**A:  No matter what, they can and do.**

Q:  I'm stubborn, I try to stay up as late as possible, though not fear based, more unconditional love based nonetheless, I get quite worried about it.

**A:  The only people needing to worry are those carrying lots of bad baggage.**

Q:  What guise is the subterranean Vrils that helped the Nazi's going under now?
Thanks.

**A:  They haven't changed their stripes much.  They flourish under tyranny and suffering, mostly found in oppressive left wing and Islamic regimes.**

Q:  Is the universe an infinite mirror such as the video below?  Infinity Mirror Illusion!:  https://www.youtube.com/watch?v=VTONKZkaVX4 Or does it ACTUALLY cover an infinite amount of space in infinite directions (concepts beyond "direction") inside/outside and beyond?!!?  I plan on making one of those soon, looks really cool:)!

**A:  The universe really is infinite; the space it occupies is the illusion.**

Q:  I was wondering what your take was on the reason why Christianity was made to take over Paganism nearly 2000 years ago?

**A:  Change is the only constant.  The Roman Empire had an expiration date as did Judaism.  Christianity preserved both for a future time.**

Q:  What do you think the world would be like now if this had never happened and all the people that are now Christian were Pagan?

**A:  The world would not be better off.  However, the time for religion has peaked and wanes.**

Q:  I think [nnnn's] problem is that Lou never seems to recognize, or speak, of this underlying life force that is "The Vine" and is the essence of who we and everything else.  The River that runs through it.  Maybe he has just never felt the need to.  I don't know, but it is something I have long wondered about as well. But I enjoyed so much of what Lou had to say regarding integrity and way of life it wasn't a big problem for me.  I would still like to know Lou's view of the fundamental spiritual concept of "The Vine" which seems to have run through almost all spiritual teachings throughout time.

A:  • "The Vine" creates a substance that intoxicates, wine.

• Wine creates courage and loosens the tongue and rewards with a hangover.

• Jesus turned water into wine without the middleman, the vine.

• Trees are taken down by vines.

• Forests are slowly decimated by vine infestations, making way for new trees.

• Human containers have roots and family trees.

• Souls, like vines, entangle and strangle the trees and roots.

• Souls are not spiritually connected to existence.

• Spirituality is a delusion cause by too much wine from the vine.

No, I haven't been drinking wine... or anything else for that matter.  I hate the after affects, headaches.

## Pg. 457 — 2011-03-09

Q:  Hey Lou good morning!  You posted once that the Jewish race came here with a privilege.  What is that privilege?  Thanks, and have a good day!

A:  **The Jews are the only race privileged to be hated and persecuted by nearly all people and nations in the history of man.  That's quite a privilege. The "why" is "highly privileged" information too.**

Q:  Hey Lou and fellow Whiners: since my "out of the blue" life changing ICU vacation, (most of which I do not remember except for wild/crazy/spacey/surreal/dreamy torture scenarios) I have drifted off self-help literature and seeking the easy way out with simple and futile religion or spirituality answers.  It was pretty easy to do.

Lou...the spirituality delusion, I got that!  And there was no huge sucking sound or void.  Thanks!  I think many of us are standing on the corner of Hollywood and Vine, BTW, a very strange place.  That vine does have a strangle hold on most and Hollywood perpetuates it.

After reading your "Chronicles" I can see how easily most history has been tampered with and misconstrued over time.  And trying to explain to others this one simple truth gets me the NO RELIGION OR POLITICS stare.  A men in black flash of amnesia...and back to the GO BEARS!  And Dance with the Stars mentality.  This is beginning not to frustrate me so much anymore.  A better attitude deflects it.

Lou, does ET shield us in this human play from our innate flawed soul intents by giving us hard knock tests in order to correct them?  Or just endure as punishment?

**A:  Our choice justified and paid for by daily actions and attitudes.**

Q:  Is it our job down here to actively change our soul's intents?

**A:  Not possible.  Acknowledge things with eyes wide shut is the best we can hope for.**

Q:  Can we do that?  How do we do that?

**A:  That's a slice of pie worth all the gold in China.  Considering that China is buying up and hording gold as if it were, well, gold; that's a lot of fortune cookies.**

Q:  Oops, time for a re-run of American Pagan...Idol .... talk about watered down musicianship.  Watched Caligula (1979) ...screen play by Gore Vidal...that dude had to have been there...one bad ass, sadistic Roman era.  Has humanity as a whole improved at all since then or?

**A:  Hollywood has never shown what Rome had to put up with, and what it was charged with doing on this planet.  People remain un-ready for that knowledge and shielded from it then and now.  The game is not over.**

Q:  Lou said: *"Souls are not spiritually connected to existence."*

Heya Lou!  Wouldn't that depend on how you define terms like "soul" and "existence"?  For example, how can anything existing not be connected to existence, unless one or both in reality were non-existent, being merely projections of mind?  This raises the question: is a mental projection existent, non-existent, neither existent nor non-existent, or neither not existent nor not non-existent?  On the other hand, maybe you mean that since souls are immaterial, they are not connected to the materiality of existence?  Oh, it's all so confusing; maybe I should drink a few Yoohoo's before reading this site.

**A:  This site gives indigestion to lots of people, notice how few sticks around?  Spirituality has been misunderstood and abused so much that few, if anyone, really knows what it is.  Nearly everyone claims to have some of it but take a look around.  Do you see any signs of it anywhere?**


Q:  Lou said: *"Spirituality is a delusion cause by too much wine from the vine."*

Well, I gave up drinking wine about 10 years ago, in exchange for someone much more intoxicating, but that's another subject.  Perhaps here you are conflating "spirituality" with "religion", Lou.  Again, it may just come down to terminology.

**A:  One can have spirituality without religion and religion without spirituality.  They are only words with whatever meaning we attach to them.  And everyone, it seems, has their own meaning – which means nothing at all but a comfort level for that particular individual.  Religion is an empty concept, so too spirituality.**


Q:  For example, my understanding is that spirituality involves the recognition and cultivation of the spirit, or soul (the in-dwelling principle), to the point of full self-awareness.

**A:  No one ever gets near self-awareness, much less full awareness.  A sliver of awareness would crush the 3D mind to oblivion.**

Q:  Thus, the basis of spirituality in this realm, for instance, would entail living a life of integrity, transcending the triple poisons of greed, hate, and ignorance, and awakening to compassionate appreciation for all life.

A:  **Attempting virtue and integrity doesn't require spirituality, religion, or a Boy Scout badge.  Everyone has the power to live a virtuous life if they "want" to, nothing else is required.**

**BTW, greed is far less an evil than envy.  I only mention that because you left envy out of your list of evils.**

Q:  Religion, on the other hand, is merely allegiance to second-hand creeds and beliefs, typically employed by TPTB for the purposes of crowd control.  Blessings!

A:  **True, but spirituality has its own TPTB; the powers that be, to appease, be they religious or new age TPTB.**

Q:  **John Lear** said: "Lou.  Any truth to that?"  Lou said: "*Actual physical "people"* told him/advised him concerning that and other dangers, he was protected supernaturally and knew it.  Hitler was primed for the mission."

Like me?

A:  **Yes John, like you.  But, don't be thinking about starting up your own Third Reich.  Oh, and BTW, Milton said he will do New York with you any time, preferably around Christmas, for his shopping spree.**

Q:  I've been off doing my homework reading through the sleeper threads and as I suspected the questions I've asked you here on this board had previously been answered and I sincerely apologize for having "wasted your time" by asking them.  The one thing you and Milton keep hammering home is that we should act with integrity, doing the right thing in everything we do.  So, being the blind squirrel I am, I decided it might be a good idea to look up the definition of the word and found it to be vaguely defined: Adherence to moral and ethical principles; soundness of moral character; honesty.

What I might deem moral and ethical, others may not have been my experience. Therefore, I'm requesting Milton to give me/us a more explicit set of guidelines to follow so I have a better chance of doing the right thing.  Thanks in advance to you and Milton and "two thumbs up" for your work.  I'm sure that I and others have benefited greatly because of it and IMO, Milton needs to give you a big fat pay raise.

PS: I'll explain how I earned my nickname in a later post.  I'm sure you'll get a kick out of it and sure doesn't mean I'm a bad ass or a bad person.

**A:  Integrity as you say is in the eye of the beholder – everyone has their own idea what it is.  Usually whatever suits us?  A simplified version of integrity is what we expect/demand from others.  We expect car mechanics not to cheat, teachers to teach, doctors to heal, and dependable babysitters.  Doing for others as we expect from them, is a good start and simple really.**

**If you have a garden and you produce more than you need and give some of that produce to friends, neighbors, and family.  Give them what you would expect from them, if they were giving produce to you, the good stuff, not the blemished stuff.**

# Pg. 458 — 2011-03-11

Q:  Does the universe need to be supported by anything such as gravity or any such things beyond gravity?  How does it stay intact?

**A:  A finite universe needs embellishments such as: gravity, dark matter, Big Bangs, and other stuff.  An infinite universe can bypass all that stuff and the physics' red tape too. How it stays intact is simple, the universe is space filled with stuff, galaxies mostly, and galaxies manage on their own.**

Q:  Lou said: "The *universe really is infinite; the space it occupies is the illusion.*"

Are all universes/places, existence infinite beyond all like that?  NOT infinite in size?  What "space" and size does it occupy?  So, it's not infinite in size inside AND outside?

**A:  It's not possible in 3D land to grasp infinity with a clause.**


Q:  Is there anything of interest in the direct center of both the north and South Pole?  Perhaps an entrance?

**A:  There is plenty of interesting going on between and the center of the poles, but no stationary entrances, or exists.**


Q:  Lou said: *"The higher dimension rules and those dimensions under fall easily into place.  It's really cool to see them on one page."*

How do they look like on one page?  Lou said: *"really cool!"*  Do you have any information you can elaborate on?  Have you been able to witness?

**A:  I said, they were cool!  So, I must have seen something.  I wish I could elaborate.**


Q:  In the Jose Escamilla video: "Moon Rising" there are some sort of beams in space that go from earth to satellites, the moon and beyond.  What exactly are they?  Space elevators?

**A:  Not space elevators.**


Q:  Are there any bodies of water (oceans) floating around in space all alone with gigantic fish, life, or any sort of environment like mountains, forest etc., with animals, life but not existing on an actual planet?  That would be insane and cool at the same time!

**A:  Everything we "think" we conceive, exists.  And, we conceive practically nothing – not even a grain of sand in an endless sandy beach.**

Q:  **John Lear**: Lou said: *"Yes John, like you.  But don't be thinking about starting up your own Third Reich.  Oh, and BTW, Milton said he will do New York with you any time, preferably around Christmas, for his shopping spree."*

Well now, first my butter flipping days should be left behind and now I can't start my own 3rd Reich?  What kind of a CS outfit is this anyway?

A:  **I know what you mean John but getting Milty to loosen up is pure hell. He kicked me in my shins once when I asked him to move his big fat bald head blocking the television, and I have a 55-inch 3D screen – got a heck of a deal on it BTW!**

Q:  Lou, does lust (sexual) exist in the upper levels, Utopia and higher?

A:  **No, they have something much better without the naughty factor.**

Q:  Is lust wrong?

A:  **Lust is not wrong – its software preloaded into human bodies and minds by the creators of humans. Lust became a problem in modern times with the dumbing down of humans.**

Q:  Like Envy or hate?

A:  **Also, software and they both get used more than all the other programs combined. No one has to use that software.  Hate and envy hurt the user first and foremost; and that is bad.**

Q:  And you've said envy is a much bigger deal than other "sins".  I feel that way to; it seems it's much easier to get rid of hate or greed than envy.  Envy is the silent killer I feel.  Could you ask Milty from me if I had a visit 2 days ago?  I remember something, an encounter, but I don't recall fear.

A:  **Not Milty, he's been laying back not doing much lately. But other entities do come into play for various reasons and desires people have.**

Q:  You have mentioned many ET Groups that have been around in the past are still in the game under different colors/guises.  What are the current guises of: the snakes mentioned in the bible?

**A:  A branch of the reptilian clan.  I don't want to give out specifics but they have their hands in everything humans are into.**


Q:  The ET's said they came in peace 10,000 years ago, but Hell be their name?  Thanks.

**A:  It's amazing using that pickup line in a bar or anywhere else works every time.  Several bad hombres use it to this day.**


Q:  Hey Lou, I have a big problem with envy.  I notice and it causes me to almost go into a state of panic, like I can't even breathe when I become really jealous of someone.  Any suggestions how I can self-improve that aspect of my life?

**A:  Everyone on this planet has an envy problem to one degree or other.  It's normal.  No matter how well-off people are on this planet they remain impoverished on some level or other and envy creeps in.  The fact is "everyone" is filthy rich, once they get to the other side.  The trick is to get there and stay there long enough to enjoy the inheritance.**


Q:  I also have some super bad anxiety attacks, for no reason it seems, when I go too far from my comfort zone like my house, for example.  It's really hard to deal with because it almost feels like I might die from not getting enough air.  It sounds stupid but I'm thinking it's from high stress over the years.  I don't have any medical problems or a history of medical problems, so I feel like I'm losing my mind...LOL.  It started happening two years ago and its hell.  Sorry to make you feel like a psychologist.  I have a good life with good friends, so I feel like a coward when it happens.

A:  Panic attacks are also common, but they vary.  Many people are good at hiding panic and some learn to live with it.  Most of the time it goes away. Like stray cats if you give them attention they hang around.


Q: Was the quake in Japan man made?

A:  No.


Q:  More events like that to come?

A:  Natural and unnatural disasters, wars, famine, plagues, birth, and death, are the only constants.

## Pg. 459 — 2011-03-14

Q:  **John Lear:** Well I don't mind dropping the butter flipping Lou, but I sure had my heart set on my own 3<sup>rd</sup> Reich.  But I guess it's 'go along to get along' time.

A:  To dish it out, there is one teeny weeny requirement – you have to be able to take it, you know, what you dish out.  Hitler had his head shaved and many disturbing experiments done to him before being turned loose on the world.  Now he has tattoos all over his body and looks really goofy.

You have some credentials for your own shot at a 3<sup>rd</sup> Reich, John, having had your entrails dissected on ATS.


Q:  Spots not going to try anything with my cigars or Cognac, is he?  I mean that would be Goodbye Charley.

A:  If you find cigars and Cognac on the other side, you have taken a wrong turn man.  Sitting around playing a harp all day on some soft white cloud sounds better.

Q:  Lou said: *"BTW, greed is far less an evil than envy.  I only mention that because you left envy out of your list of evils."*

I'm attempting to wrap my mind around that.  Can you please elaborate?

**A:  Everyone has greed and envy.  When we call greed on someone, we usually have envy in our own souls – whether we admit to it or not.  What people end up with in their lives, on their plate, is really no one's' concern or business, and is put there by non-humans.  We don't get bothered much by those that have less than we, but we get bothered by those who have more than me.**

Q:  The first thought that comes to mind is that greed can directly affect people close to us, if our greed prevents them from sharing what we have.

**A:  What others have, has no bearing on what we have.  Everything is given or taken by invisible forces (higher beings).  Prosperity and poverty are never by chance, always deliberate and created by the same beings.**

Q:  However, envy doesn't necessarily affect those around us, if we don't actually act on our envy (I.E., it can be OK to feel a little jealous, as long as that emotion doesn't control us).

**A:  Envy is the root of hate.  A good example is the parable of Cain and Able.  Most never go that far but envy makes us unhappy and that is the real curse.**

Q:  So, are you implying that envy is worse than greed?  If it's actually acted on, and we act negatively towards the folks that we envy?  Or, are you implying that envy is always worse than greed?  If the latter's the case, then please do explain the reasoning behind that.

**A:  Hate and envy never have to be "acted on" to do damage to our own souls.  Every day that we give in to ill feelings, adds to collateral damage, mostly subtle.**

We should all be more "greedy" for the good things in life and "never" worry about "other" people's greed.  A good life depends on taking care of what is on your own plate and not what is on your brother's plate, less we rise up with rage and kill our brother, and in so doing "forever injure" our own redemption.

Q:  Hi Lou!  Still here trying to learn!  Last month after the uprising in Egypt and then on some other Islamic countries, I thought that maybe the "let's get more relaxed living" clan had something to do with it.  But then I thought that the other clan (the one that wants more miserable conditions of living), would make its move on other side of the chessboard (sort to speak).  So now we have a large part of Japan devastated by this horrible Earthquake.  Are these events "facilitated" by E.T. Factions or my imagination is on overdrive?

A:  **What is going on in the Middle East is by the same ET faction as the Japan tsunami, the Christchurch, New Zealand quake, and Australian floods.**


Q:  Hi Lou.  The thing about every object a person sees in their life being created for them.  Is this to guide people?

A:  **It's for people to stumble on, fall, and hit their nose, lest there be any confusion during interrogations at the pearly gates.**


Q:  Is the environment we enjoy mostly (urban/country) to do with a person's soul or the package they're in?

A:  **A person's package; body, mind and circumstances, projects a whole bunch of what that soul is about and where it might be going for its next gig. This life is only a rehearsal. For many, a bad rehearsal.**

Q:  Lou said: *"A branch of the reptilian clan.  I don't want to give out specifics.
It's amazing using that pickup line in a bar or anywhere else works every time.
Several bad hombres use it to this day."*

Is there anything you can disclose about what they are up to nowadays or what
their agenda is?  Thanks.

**A:  Snakes give and take as is evident in our daily news.  How many people
wake up by all the horrific noise on this planet?  Not many at all.  People are
tough nuts to crack, down here.**

Q:  **John Lear**: Lou, on Friday morning at 8:35 I saw the ignition of the Ichihara
refinery with what appeared to be a bright blue beam, identical to the beam that
was present at the BP gulf disaster.  All CNN videos after that clipped off the top
of that video or used a zoom to hide the beam that I saw.

**A:  Just keep it under your tinfoil hat, John.  "They" don't let children play
with matches.  OK, they did let "the buck stops here" Harry Truman from
Missouri, play with the atom bomb over Japan via "Oppenheimer", and the
proliferation of atomic bombs with the Soviet Union.  What is going on now
is beyond human tinkering and blue beam tech without a clause. Well, ok,
"they" still tinker.**

Q:  Thanks Lou, now I am worried that those guys are on the move.  Any hints
on how to pass up the good vibe?

**A:  No point in worrying.  They have always been on the move, more or
sometimes less.  Tsunamis of ignorance are the worst kinds of disasters,
plaguing much of the world lately, yet they never make a splash on the news
networks.  A virtuous life is the best defense.**

## Pg. 460 — 2011-03-15

Q:  Lou, you are on the mark that Japans earthquake was not man made, but from
outside forces playing around.  Now my question is, this was done because even
that looks like a bad thing and in the long run it will be a good thing?  What I

mean is that if this didn't happen right now, later on it would have been more massive and problematic with more consequences and deaths?  Like choosing to sacrifice some for the good of the rest or this was caused because some ET's were having 4 of July fireworks between factions?

**A:  None of the above.**

So, Spot drinks very often Lou??  haha I mean should John start to save his Cognac in safe places around the world?  Like Noah's ark, but of the wines LOL heheehe.

**A:  Spot doesn't drink at all; he can hardly hold his Yoohoo's.**


Q:  So, what have been on Milton, still relaxing I mean working?  Hehehe, sounds like Milton has become a potato couch type of ET lately, and looks like he's enjoying it.  Hehee.  If he comes to Mexico for tacos or burritos or tequila tell him to pay me a visit.  Have great day everybody!

**A:  Milton's been standing at the door, popcorn, and drink in hand since last night waiting for the movie "Paul", to hit the theaters.  I told him it was 3 days till Friday, but he doesn't care.**


Q:  Lou said: *"They prefer calling it what it is, dimensions and such.  But even dimensions are not correct."*

So, are you saying dimensions are not dimensions but we call them dimensions because they are dimensions!?

**A:  With the appropriate "prospective" we can know and understand dimensions.  Appropriate being the key.**


Q:  Do all solar systems work by all the planets within revolving around the mother star?

**A:  No.**

Q:  Say, if any random person were able to view a planet, such as Mars or Uranus would ET camouflage everything?

A:  **Yes.**


Q:  Another dimension?

A:  **It's done with mirrors.  Look what magicians have been able to pull off with sleight of hand, mirrors, and cute women scantily dressed to distract attention.  After all, we all have short attentions spans when it comes to sex objects.**


Q:  Some of the deepest parts of the oceans such as the Mariana trench and the Puerto Rico trench, what is down there?

A:  **Marine life.**


Q:  Lou said: *"All the beauty and awesome things we have down here only compare to a baby rattle only a few notches up on Utopia planets.  Beyond Utopia there is no ceiling and awe can't touch what is going on."*

Have you experienced the awe way up there?  Any information?

A:  **You must see for yourself to really appreciate, words fail. And yes.**


Q:  Lou said: *"Gods don't come down to sandbox level, they hire mercenaries."*

Is Milton one of those mercenaries?  Where do the Gods "chill"?

A:  **I'm having trouble visualizing Milty, popcorn in hand, standing at the door and spilling his drink on the floor, as a mercenary.  Then again...**


Q:  Greetings Lou, you have noted the same ET Faction is responsible for all the issues in the Middle East, the Japan problem, and the various other places.  What exactly is the point of their involvement here to cause these issues for us?

**A:  They have rained death and destruction on this planet for eons.  The reasons vary and their abilities do too.**

Q:  Are these trigger tests for vast population blocks?

**A:  For the whole world, who watch in awe like sheep with wolves in their midst.**

Q:  Also, the events in Japan are really starting to look grim; multiple nuke reactors and such on melt down.  How far are they going to take this?

**A:  The world did not come to an end with BP in the Gulf – this too will pass with some scars.**

Q:  Is this same ET Faction part of the renegade sorts?

**A:  Of sorts.**

Q:  And if that is the case, is the opposite side ET's going to counteract some of the unfolding events?  Thanks!

**A:  Nonstop.  The hidden background is a busy place, always.**

Q:  Lou said: *"The hidden background is a busy place, always."*
Heya Lou!  Would it be fair to say that Plus and Minus are co-dependent dance programs running in perpetual search for zero (union), eternally performing their synchronized numbers against a background of perfect zero (silent awareness) Blessings!

**A:  Only on the lower end of existence, where Earth lies does chasing the tails apply.  The Yin and Yang hide, and the infinity of Pi leaves mathematicians dreary eyed.  Awareness is never silent upstairs, the party animals.**

Q: Hi Lou. I wanted to ask a few questions. One about Japan. The ones responsible for the world's abuse and hardships, the Middle East, are they not the S group? Are they not connected to the underground DUMBS, and the cloning programs/abductions? Are they not also connected to Elenin and that planet/object bigger than Jupiter somewhere on the outskirts of the solar system? Someone posted elsewhere that, the same conditions that caused Japan's situation, is responsible for the activity at Yellow Stone. He said he was a scientist and of course, our science is completely off. He was suggesting that changes that had been expected at the end of May were now going to occur, March, relatively soon. I was told several months ago that this wasn't known for sure, but April/May/June, and then October. But North America would bear the brunt of widening at the equator or some earth changes, to the north end. This had to do with Elenin's gravity, and that they hadn't figured in its size, I think.

A: **Anyone can throw a dart and hit on a disaster or two. But the "root cause" and effect, not so.**

Q: My second question is about Elenin, and some Russian report about it being intelligently controlled by, I believe that large object outside or just within the solar system. And that this is a cyclical event. That this is relating to destructions. That this is related to the S group or renegades, the ones doing things here, bullies. Is this report in any way true?

A: **Like in the bible, there is some truth in that report but little substance. BTW, I haven't read the report only what you have mentioned here.**

Q: The part about greed and envy. I don't truly understand that one too much. I know greed is a big part of some people's agendas. I guess it's more about ambition, not seeing others in need, being service-to-self, and distractions. So, the objects are like, in the Bible they talk about the weeds and things that choke the good seed. Note, I can interpret the bible, but I don't like the wars and negative things mentioned in it. I can see light things in it, but that's true of most writings, there are mixtures. I do believe in what Yeshua modeled as the way, which was seeing past the world, nothing in it mattered, it matters but not as a goal.  That it's about love, and service-to-others.

**A:  The word "greed" is a political term, used very effectively to dumb down the masses and make them envious of others.**

Q:  The idea of the pearly gates, and karma, everything in your life being there showing your next steps.  I don't agree with that at all.  That is something no one can judge at all, and in reality, the tests and circumstances are not just about us.  Some people roll up their sleeves and head for the trenches, and lose themselves hoping to find themselves, to reach family.

**A:  Most hate castor oil but it does the job, so does karma.**

Q:  We're not here to ignore those in need, but to be true adults, try to grow up more.  Adults serve children, they don't rule over them or ignore them, and we're trying to grow up more here.  Love is the most important force there is.  So, greed and envy, well anything opposite to Love would be the tests.  Love is anything that is not us.  That is the best definition, someone said that it's the other.  But I would imagine this is less about Greed and more about having power over people.  The power of love versus the love of power!

**A:  To find the neediest people one need only look in the mirror.  A sick person doesn't heal other sick people.  Nevertheless, there is nothing wrong and everything right with helping others as a way of helping "ourselves" in the process.  The gods do the heavy lifting; but some people like taking the credit.**

Q:  So, are people really supposed to think everyone is getting what they deserve, and attend to their own personal lives?

**A:  It's certainly easier to help clean and point out other peoples' messy house/lives, than to look at our own mess and have to dig through it and clean it up.**

Q:  I've experienced Family, and my own family, where there is no time.  One thing I know, when people wake up, which usually after they pass over, they just want to get back and help their loved ones, the ones they were aware of, no matter how hard their lives were.

A:  **Guilt is a trip we take with us to the other side, for squandering what we could have, should have, done/achieved while here.**


Q:  You word things carefully, so I'm not sure that the things you've said mean you're saying not to help, I don't want to jump the gun on assuming it actually.  I know you've written that we're not here to change the world, but the world changes us.  That makes sense in a way, but also, if we're not trying to change ourselves, family, and make a difference in the world, if we're able to, and if those circumstances are given, but struggling or asking, yearning to do so, is that not a part of the tests too?

A:  **Getting up every morning is the biggest test.**


Q:  While Love and STO is growing up, how much love does Family above, (where there is no measurement therefore no real above, but a metaphor) do they have?  I have experienced that this is an incredible amount.  Forgiveness of self and others is especially important; it's part of our tests.  It's also a part of growing up?

A:  **We have the capacity to show the same love down here as they do upstairs.  The difference is we pick and choose and sometimes focus it in the wrong places.  Plus, we let ego and attitude get in the way "all" the time.**


Q:  How logical or ethical or caring would it be if people go through these tests, only to have the vast majority constantly falling into regression and pain and suffering?

**A:  We have so much family on the other side that we hardly notice those that remain struggling down below.  Partially kidding.  Children struggle, but eventually they get through it and become adults.  Some take longer than others.**

Q:  School or prison?  Fallen or a part of the journey in infinity, these lessons?

**A:  All of the above**

Q:  The large round shape that was on Soho some time ago.  It was big, much bigger than earth, near the sun.  I would imagine this could something intelligently controlled as well.  Does this relate to Elenin and that other larger object?

**A:  You mean like lining up a billiard shot?**

Q:  Hi Lou, so, is that why evil people whether tyrants like Hitler or renegades with lots of power are allowed to mess with the world because they have or can endure everything they unleash?  And what was the purpose of the experiments done on Hither?

**A:  Qualifications and experiences are valuable tools in any occupation one chooses or is forced into.**

Q:  And regarding your other drip about this life for most being a rehearsal for the next one and that our personality/life/body being clues, are there any specifics you can disclose; such as, things that indicate either moving to better things or worse?  Thanks.

**A:  Regardless of what we look like to ourselves or others, how we treat ourselves and others on a regular basis is a big tip off, of where the hell, or not, we are going from here.  Cleaning up our act so that we can better ourselves sounds like an old record, worn out cliché.  Nevertheless, it works.**

[Q:  Greetings Lou, you have noted the same ET Faction is responsible for all the issues in the Middle East, the Japan problem, and the various other places.  What exactly is the point of their involvement here to cause these issues for us?]

In response to the above, Lou said: *"They have rained death and destruction on this planet for eons.  The reasons vary and their abilities do too"*.

This response made me think of Roman/Greek Mythology and the "gods" varied abilities and limitations.  Is there a connection Sleeper/Lou?

**A:  Much of myth is rooted in delusional reality, or life as we know it or think we know it.  Delusional reality is what religions, science, and political paradigms operate on, now and in the past.  Myths were as real then as the illusions we exist under today.**


Q:  Hello Lou, Is the incident with the nuclear reactor in Japan a sign of new safer technology coming through to replace nuclear energy for powering cities?  Do you see anything new and safer on the horizon in this department?

**A:  We literally swim in "free" energy, bathed by the sun, blown from the wind, and waves from water.  The catch is to harness energy in large quantities and store it somewhere.  That's time consuming and expensive... for humans.**

**There are a few things on the drawing board but nothing that will alleviate the need for massive amounts of energy we consume daily. Not in the near future.**


Q:  You have mentioned in the past how nuclear power was given to us to get us to the next stage in powering the cities for larger amounts of people.  I don't think I would like to be a Nuclear Power Plant Salesman at the moment.......LOL

**A:  Nuclear power has never been loved, but for now it remains the only thing for industrialized countries.  The alternative is we could turn off our heating and cooling, drink from streams and go back to living in huts.**

Q:  If the renegades really wanted to hurt Milton, what would he do if they destroyed the Yoo-hoo factories?

**A:  Lucky for Milty, bob put up the recipe for making Yoohoo's.  But this Yoo-hoo, me, is not going to cook up Yoohoo's for Milty should the Yoo-hoo factories get blown up.  Milty tried cooking something in the kitchen once, it escaped and is now living in the walls.  Needless to say, I don't let Milty in the kitchen anymore.**

Q:  Hey Lou!  Any truth on this?  Www.ufocasebook.com/2011/finalword.html

**A:  Humans have never controlled this planet.**


Q:  Also, I watched this video.  UFO seen over Brazil this week: https://www.youtube.com/watch?time_continue=1&v=JrXdcQeIrs8 It seemed the UFO was performing something similar to the one caught on video in Jerusalem.  I don't know if it's fake or not.  Any comments?  Thanks man!

**A:  Neat video!**

Q:  Hello Dear LOU!  Question about death.  Did renegades take people's lives before time comes for some as in this massive event?  I mean, do they care if is time to leave for somebody or no?  Hope I explain well myself.

May I write in Spanish this question?  I hope my Mexican friends help with translation.  Please?  Izarit o alguien mas?  Lo que quiero preguntar es que si todos tenemos el tiempo de nuestra muerte marcado,como lo ha dicho Lou, cuando ocurren los eventos masivos de muertes como el actual de Japon, y los Renegados lo han producido, ellos se llevan a los que ya cumplieron su estadia en este planeta, los cuales podrian morir de todas maneras, o se van personas que no habian terminado su ciclo?  Los Renegados lo harian con el fin de dañar a la gente o a alguien mas?  Si es asi, que hacen nuestros guias o los guias de las personas que son afectadas por ellos?  Gracias Por favor pregunten si no queda claro aun en español!  Espero no estar violando alguna regla del foro.

[Pablo's translation: What I want to ask is, if the time of our deaths are all fixed, as Lou has said.  When massive deaths occur from catastrophes, such as in the recent Japanese event produced by the Renegades; do they only take those who are ready to die on this planet or does it include others who haven't finished their life-cycle?  Would the Renegades do it in order to harm anyone?  If so, what role do our guides play?]

**A:  Nobody gets taken even by renegades until their time is up.  Sometimes the renegades are allowed to take those belonging to them sooner.  Those not belonging to the renegades are taken by "other" entities monitoring the situation.**

## Pg. 462 — 2011-03-18

Q:  Lou, now it seems countries are scared and calling for the end of nuclear energy, like Germany.  You once said that people were scared of it in the past, and that made the technology not evolve, and it was too bad because nuclear energy could help us advance.  I wonder if one the intents of whoever created the Japan disaster was this.

**A:  Nuclear bombs have saved millions of lives by keeping the superpowers in check during the cold war, more or less, mostly more.**

**Nuclear energy has saved millions of lives by reducing poisonous emissions from smokestacks burning coal that suffocated large industrial cities during the last century.  Not to mention all the coal miners dying digging for that nasty coal.  The sane truth never makes the headlines.  Crap and paranoia sell papers and controls peoples' attitudes.**

Q:  Thank you, I think our lives clue us into a lot, but we must never stop trying to help others, even though the things everyone here goes through are temporal, this hell-zone is so bad just witnessing what others to others, I've refused to budge and walk forward many times growing up, because just one of these things, makes the universe and all of existence disappear and have spent some time arguing about this world.  I believe in healing not corporeally harming people who have been hurt.  This is a lifetime, since teenage years, of sensing that team and saying no.  But I also got answers, in the end relating to progression, and sensed there was no other way, but no one should go through what people do here.  There are things here that make everything in existence vanish for me.  Also, that we shouldn't focus on ourselves at all.

I think your answers are quite balanced though.


Q:  About the ET situation and the link above concerning Assange, and ET takeover by 2015 or so.  I realize this planet has always been like this, but is there a more visible presence coming?

A:  **In olden times the emergence, the presence of a "superior"  power such as Rome, sent terror throughout the land, and for good reason, it meant the end for the primitive people that were conquered, annihilated and sometimes assimilated into the new order.  It was never pretty.**

**There are "Alien" beings salivating to make themselves "publicly" known to the inferior human race.  So far, they have been kept in check and the plan is to keep it that way.**


Q:  In my questions you said that the report had some truth but no substance.  Are there sides in this issue then?  Something different than what's being said perhaps, we're getting the wrong information?

A:  **The information is almost always wrong unless it comes from foaming-at-the-mouth, Spot (Milton).**

**There is much disinformation out there and like every other belief thrown at us we have to pick and choose or ignore it and watch something funny on the tube.**


Q:  When I was meditating it was like being pulled to that object and it seemed more like a craft appearing like a planetoid on the surface, but it was a craft.

A:  **If "they" really want you to know about this mysterious object, why not just tell you, show you, and be done with it?  Milty showed me his ship, I puked for a week after, but I think it was because the Yoo-hoos in his frig that I drank had gone sour.  I can't stand the stuff to this day!**

There are oodles of ships out in space, some heading our way some leaving for good.  Troop rotations and such.  Hopefully, the new crop will be as nice and subtle as the old guard.

Q:  If your navigating family problems at home, for example, surrounded by some negative people and rarely listened to, and yet you are nudged to help locally or abroad or bring light to homelessness for example, is it ego to not wait until your lives are perfect in order to assist?

A:  Helping others is always a good thing, I've never said otherwise.  But I have said that helping others helps the helper more, does anyone deny that?

Q:  Hey Milty...anybody you know?  Paul – Trailer 2: https://www.youtube.com/watch?v=16Jfld1-kOI

A:  Milton doesn't think there is room for two smart ass ET's on this planet. I agree.  I never go to a movie when it first comes out and may not see this one for a while.  Milty's popcorn has gone stale and most of his drink is on my floor.  I hate to break the news to him that we're not going to see Paul tonight.  Thanks for the trailers!  Milty just stuffed stale popcorn up my nose.  There is nothing worse than a pissed ET!!!

Q:  Hey Lou, how are you doing?  Has crabby Milton stopped by lately?  I'm enjoying the nice weather, bowling, and having a nice vodka and sprite. Appreciation.

A:  Yeah, the crab is here, you should see the steam coming out his ears right now.  I think he's going to blow up or something.

Q:  Hey Sleeper (Lou), thanks for all the latest input.  Sometimes I just sit and wonder, with my mouth wide open.

A:  Are you up for some stale popcorn?

Q:  Lou said: *"Regardless what we look like to ourselves or others, how we treat ourselves and others on a regular basis is a big tip off of where the hell, or not, we are going from here.  Cleaning up our act so that we can better ourselves seems like an old record, a worn-out cliché.  Nevertheless, it works."*

Lou, I understand about not treating others badly, treating them better than we would expect ourselves to be treated, but how would someone treat themselves badly?  Would examples of treating ourselves badly be: wallowing in self-pity, embracing misery, seeing the glass as half-empty, basically having a negative outlook on life?

A:  **"Embracing misery" may be up there, self-mutilation, drugs and too much Vodka.  Also reading some of my posts and watching my YouTube videos could be cruel and unusual punishment.**

Q:  What do you make of conscientious objectors who refuse military service or work in armaments factories on pacifistic grounds etc., but are prepared to undertake any other role to be of service but not hurt the enemy in times of national crisis, I.e., ambulance driver, raging forest fire fighter and so on. Thanks.

A:  **Most people are not cut out for combat and should be allowed to do other things if they so choose.**

Q:  Hi Lou, how are you today?  You never cease to amaze me by saying so much true things by using just a few words.

You are so right here.  I must admit that I did realize that no earlier than after reading what you said there [about Nuclear bombs].  But don't you think it's possible that it could go this time very wrong; I mean that something as a meltdown could occur, or will that not be allowed to happen?

A:  **Nuclear energy is not a toy and will be respected or else there are consequences.  Space exploration is extremely dangerous, and humans will encounter many unimagined obstacles and life-threatening ordeals in the** coming century, that's called progress.  If it weren't for people like John and other test pilots we would be forced to drive on unsafe highways, sinkable ships to cross oceans, and crummy railroad trains.  All that stuff comes with improvements over time.

Those who do only safe things do nothing at all.

Q:  Or do you find that paranoia from my side?

A:  Yes.  We are not here on earth to be safe.  We are here to push the envelope, get in a few laughs, and die.  And if we did it right, then the fun starts, if not, we are back in the danger zone.

Q:  By the way, I am now translating the last chapter.  (10)

A:  Cool!

Q:  Lou said: *"If it weren't for people like John and other test pilots we would be forced to drive on unsafe highways, sinkable ships to cross oceans, and crummy railroad trains."*
I do realize that very well Lou, and that is why I have so much respect for you as well as for people like John and other test pilots and so many others.

Lou said: *"Those who do only safe things do nothing at all."*  I do realize even that also very well Lou, therefore I realize myself very well, that I belong to those who do regarding that nothing at all.

A:  Some people pushed envelops in previous lives and climbed impossible mountains and are here now to tidy up a few things and enjoy life.  The clue is in the "relative harmony" such people experience in their present lives. Present being the key word. As in gift.

Q:  Lou said: *"Embracing misery" may be up there, self-mutilation, drugs and too much Vodka.  Also reading some of my posts and watching my YouTube videos could be cruel and unusual punishment."*

Well I guess I must be a sadomasochist then because I love reading your posts and watching your vids.  On a more serious note, my older sister kind of hammers the booze, drugs and misery, she seems to lurch from one disaster or crisis to the next, she never seems happy or settled and I'm so very, very worried about her.

I have finally contacted my mum after 15 years.  I've been meeting her, and things are going great, my sister will not even entertain the idea of coming with me to see her and she can't get her head around the fact that I am.  I'm so very worried about my sister, but I don't know how to help her.  I understand what you were saying about sick people not being able to heal other sick people, so maybe I'm not the best person to help her, but I want to try –  I just don't know where to start.

I'm also ashamed to say that I have been kind of avoiding her lately.  I feel bad that my life is relatively good while hers is in a total mess.

A:  **Family, friends and invisible entities are not enough to get our personal lives in order.  Ultimately, we have to climb down into our own hellish pit, filled with vipers, old tires, gunk and who knows what else we might have dumped into it through the years.  Very little warm sunshine reaches inside the pit.  Once in the pit, only personal effort and determination will get us out.  Always nice to keep a sturdy ladder handy and use wisely any handout you receive.**

Q:  Lou you answer most of it, but the last part about renegades harming people and guides I would like to hear your inputs please.  Grants translation of Frami's Spanish (above):  "What I want to ask is if everybody has their time marked, like Lou has said, when massive deaths occur from catastrophes, such as Japan, and the renegades produced them, do they take those who have completed their time on Earth, or are people who have not completed their life cycle also taken?"

**A: Those that belong to the renegades (sold their souls to evil and ignorance) can be taken before their cycle is over.**

Q: Do the renegades do this to hurt these people, or someone else?

**A: Those left behind, survivors, are left to deal with many issues. Those that died will go to their destinations, destinations determined by their life actions before death took them away. It doesn't matter who or what killed them.**

Q: If it's like that, what do our guides or the guides of the people that have been affected do?

**A: After a human dies, "other" beings hash out the details of their destination, not the renegades. Unless a soul has given itself over to hate and darkness.**

Q: [Adam] Hi Lou, you mentioned that Milton has known all of us in previous lives. Can you tell me if he was my father, schoolteacher or maybe my mailman? If he was my wife, did he look cute in an apron and does he cook? Maybe there is room for him here if he cooks? I already have a wife, but she doesn't cook. My neighbors will not mind, they are all Mormon and wish they had more wives.

**A: I don't know if Milton is being a smart-ass, but he said he doesn't know you from Adam.**

## Pg. 464 — 2011-03-21

Q: Not at all. They are more like your own brand of Zen, and we, as watchers of this ordinariness, experience a kind of "Chop-Wood-Carry-Water" sort of thing. It is a sharing of what takes the form of some of what is in your everyday. And a perfect example of what is being ever-manifested from living with and around the 'needs' of this fleshy envelope of earth's corporeality, and man's constant 'man-euverings' while being in residence.

**A:  I use a chainsaw to chop my wood.  But that feller Zen doesn't help me carry the wood out of the forest.  Milty poured some of his Yoo-hoo into my chain saw once, said it works better than the smelly gasoline.  I don't let him help me chop wood anymore.**

Q:  Lou said: *"Those who do only safe things do nothing at all.  We are not here on earth to be safe, we are here to push the envelope, get in a few laughs, and die.  And if we did it right, then the fun starts, if not were back in the danger zone."*

So, what would be considered pushing the envelope?  I imagine that it's different for each individual depending on why they are here, and their present circumstances, but can you give me some examples, please Lou?

**A:  Like you said it's different for everyone.  Pushing the envelope is doing things we would rather not do.  Rock our own boat or the boat of friends and family, which often comes with consequences.  Sometimes consequences are good in the long run.**

Q:  Oh, and tell Milty that I'm not trying to squeeze the test answers out of you, I'm just...errr..curious!  Also, if he still desperately wants to go to the movies, I'll take him, as long as he buys some fresh popcorn.

**A:  Fresh popcorn?  Milton loves his popcorn aged and stale, like my jokes**

Q:  Lou said: *"There are "Alien" beings salivating to make themselves "publicly" known to the inferior human race.  So far they have been kept in check and the plan is to keep it that way."*

What do these beings want from humans that they already can't just take?

**A:  Peace of mind.  Once the cat is out of the bag, it ain't going back in.**

Q:  **John Lear**: So, in 40 years when: Those in denial are dead.  Those who grew up hearing about aliens are adults the alien appears; it will be no big deal.  Whereas the supposed 'disclosure' today would create a lot of problems for a lot of people?

A:  **Disclosure would create a lot of problems for "all" people no matter how much some believe they are ready.**

**During abductions people are placed into controlled mental states and still crap their pants and remain uncomfortable for the duration even after their diapers are changed.  There are exceptions to that rule but nevertheless higher beings in their "natural state" do not mix well with humans.**

**Full disclosure is not in the works.  Some disclosure happens now and then but gets covered up quickly.**


Q:  **John Lear**: Lou, Spot oozed in yesterday morning and said if I didn't take him to Paul (the movie) he would take me to Saturn and let me have total recall.  Since I didn't feel like puking for week, I took him along with my wife Marilee and my grandson Damien.

A:  **Good move on your part John, total recall is a bloody mess, I saw the movie.**


Q:  John Lear: If you loved the Three Stooges and know all about Aliens this is the movie for you.  My wife Marilee worked in several Three Stooges movies, loves them, and sometimes listens to my stuff.  So, she went bonkers watching Paul.  It made my heart happy to see her laughing so hard.  Whereas me and Damien sat like lumps watching stuff that was boring and endless and once we had finished the popcorn had nothing to do.  Spot was a writhing lump of giggles and Marilee and he made total asses out of themselves rolling around and ho-ho-ho-ing at every little remark.

I should tell you at this point that I am slightly deaf.  It's not that I can't hear, it's that I cannot understand what people are saying so I miss 99% percent of the sotto voces, and 80% of the rest.  The only thing I thought was kinda funny was when Paul and everybody were sitting around the campfire and Paul lights up a joint and passes it around.

For any sane persons like Damien and myself the movie was a Dud with a capital D.  When the movie was finished, I had to carry Spot on my shoulders out to the car as he was still laughing and giggling.  I told him he was nuts and he 'playfully' whacked me in the side of the head.  You know what that's like, right?

**A:  When Spot whacks me upside the head it's not playful, John, I'm jealous.**

Q:  Anyway, when we got to my house he told me he had to get back to 'Lou's Place' before you polished off all of the Yoohoo's.  Did you notice that he was gone?

**A:  Fat chance of me polishing off his Yoohoo's.  No, I never miss Spot.**

Q:  Here is a photo of Marilee and Adam West in the Three Stooges movie, "The Gunslinger":

[broken link]

**A:  Nice, but where are the stooges?**

Q:  **John Lear**: Hello Lou, this is your forum and you can say anything you want, but I think making fun of Mr.  Zen is way out of line.  Mr.  Zen (don't know his first name) is a really cool dude and has shown many, many, many persons how to live their lives and how to have sex properly.

**A:  Since you put it that way John, I might have to read up on this dude Zen.**

Q:  Chop wood, carry water is a euphemism for living life with integrity; and without envy, hate or greed.  But instead of living your life WIAWEHG you 'chop wood and carry water'.

**A:  Spot got his euphemism stuck in his zipper once.**

Q:  Most people I know, however, order wood by the half cord and get their water at Water Windmill where you fill up your own 5-gallon container.

**A:  Ordering wood by the cord is the easy road, we all know where that gets us!  Besides, what the hell am I going to do with all that dead wood I have in my hidden garden if I don't chop it up every fall?**

Q:  But chop wood, carry water is a great pickup line and works most of the time. When I parted company with one of the ladies I had used the line on, she told me (actually yelled at me): "Why don't you chop your thing off and see if any water comes out you moron".  She was unhappy at something, but I don't know what.

**A:  Yikes!**

Q:  So, if you don't want to A-L-I-E-N-A-T-E (get it?) half the people on this forum I would take it easy on Mr.  Zen.  He is very popular around Hollywood, like up in Topanga Canyon and places like that.  Just a 'heads up'.

**A:  Thanks for the heads-up John!  I mentioned Zen to Spot once and Spot lifted up his leg, so I slowly backed out of the room.  Personally, Zen sounds like a nice enough fellow from what you've said.**

Q:  Hi Lou!  This is a great documentary [missing].  What do you think about that?

**A:  Great, Milty now wants to be a vigilante.  I told him that vigilantes are looking for freaky entities like him and if they found him, they would take away his Yoohoo's.  Now he's pissed!**

Q: There's been reports of loud rumbling noises in LA, San Diego, Florida, New York. So, what are these LOUD noises in the following videos? HAARP? Underground construction? Pretty creepy if you ask me. [Video link bad]

Noise goes on for about 8 minutes and a big flash explodes! The noise then stops, and it begins to rain *Found it on ATS so I don't want the credit for finding this.

Www.abovetopsecret.com/forum/thread677482/pg1

www.abovetopsecret.com/forum/thread677757/pg1

I don't think this has been asked but have you visited deep down, DEEP down in the caverns of Earth? What's it like if you've been there? That would make an awesome adventurous book!

**A: Yes, I have been to hell down below. Who has time to write books? Especially books with a sliver of a niche.**

Q: Lou said: *"Some people think Earth is a zoo, Mars is a bigger zoo."*

How so, any detailed description?

**A: Zoos here are nice, tame, and safe, more or less. On Mars there are much more bizarre creatures – not tame or safe, tricky, spooky, and clever.**

Q: And don't we? Excuse me, I mean TPTB have outpost's and "stuff" up there?

**A: Of course, why? Don't humans believe this stuff?**

Q: Hey Lou, hope you are all good in the hood. As I was sitting here on my chair reading away and cruising the web I felt a small tickle on my neck and brushed it off as nothing, but then looked down 2 minutes later to find a small brown spider on my arm rest. Instantly I freaked out and jumped out my seat like a little girl.

Why are people like me so afraid of spiders do you think? That question is almost more mysterious to me than a lot of other things. Needless to say, I killed the little bugger...just feels like instinct. Why do creepy crawlies bother some people so much, it's embarrassing. Maybe someone gets a good chuckle though.

**A: Just think if that spider were as big as you and could manipulate your world; spin you in a web of strange dimensions and you be powerless to do anything about it.**

**In the movies, humans are superior to "Alien beings". In real life, humans have Zero defense when ET's are in our space/room. We get freaked out by little bugs because "all" have seen the big bugs in dream land, the real land. Nevertheless, guides have a can of Raid, and sometimes use it.**

## Pg. 466 — 2011-03-23

Q: Oh OK, I think I get what you're saying to a degree. Big bugs don't sound like my cup of tea, that's for sure. Are there any ''nice'' big bugs? Or are we all scared of them for a reason? I've heard of people having encounters with giant 7 ft tall or more Praying Mantises in their bedroom and on UFO's...no wonder people crap their pants during abductions and what not. I don't think people could handle that in 1000 years from now, let alone 40.

**A: There are nice big bugs and nice and not so nice small bugs that get under our skin. It's a buggy world with far too many creepy crawlies. That's why living in huts sucks. Technologically, bug and weather resistant homes are better. Once here we can't so easily choose where we will live, and some will get bugged more than others.**

Q: Hey Lou Good Morning! Mars inhabitants, humanoid type? I read once they look Asian, Mongolian type to be more specific.

**A: Humanoids inhabit Mars, several types, and hairy ones too.**

Q:  Is Mars a prison-planet also?

A:  **It has prisons and isolation/storage chambers.  Also, plenty of freedom for some.**

Q:  Once we get to Mars, are we going to "discover "their civilization or it will be hidden from us?  Thanks, Lou.

A:  **We haven't discovered a whole lot of freaky things we sometimes rub elbows with here on Earth.  Blinders are easily applied to the masses too smart to believe in the paranormal stuff.**

Q:  **John Lear**: Marilee is on the left.  (pic link bad)

A:  **Yup, that's them, the masters of the universe.  Eat your heart out MENSA people.  Sour grapes you say?  Well I was a straight F student in grade school from all the hooky I played, never went to Junior or High school.  Yeah, I turned my sour grapes into whine, I mean wine.**

Q:  John, I agree, "Paul" was OK.  Who was it on board who recommended "The Adjustment Bureau" That film resonated.  Sleeper, I would love to read your review of that one.

A:  **The Adjustment Bureau?  When does it come out?  I'll Google it.  More time I don't get to spend in my garden.**

Q:  Here in Arizona we do have lots of Alien Raids....but I don't think it is what Milton is talking about.

A:  **I'm an illegal alien, didn't become a citizen until after I came out of the military, and still had my green card.  OK, I wasn't illegal; my parents came to America legally – I procrastinated before making my citizenship official.  The military believes I'm an "illegal alien" from another planet.  But that's**

**another story should I ever get around to writing it. It's difficult not to play hooky when the weather gets nice.**


Q: Lou said: *"Alien beings salivating to make themselves publicly known to the inferior human race. So far they have been kept in check and the plan is to keep it that way."*

I thought this is why there is reality TV, for the Aliens to make themselves known. What about the Kardashians?

**A: The Kardawhat? I've done my Google search for the day. I'm trying to cut down, way down.**

Q: Lou said: *"I use a chainsaw to chop my wood. But that feller Zen, doesn't help me carry the wood out of the forest. Milty poured some of his Yoo-hoo into my chain saw once, said it work better than the smelly gasoline. I don't let him help me chop wood anymore."*

Oh my, Milty is sometimes just too capricious – especially with such mischievous tastes 'fueling' his proclivities.

**A: I'm glad John took Milty to see Peter, Paul, and Mary. I can't hardly stand or sit through a movie even if it's a great movie. Milton still picking stale popcorn out his teeth. Capricious and disturbing.**


Q: Lou said: *"Pushing the envelope is doing things we would rather not do. Rock our own boat or the boat of friends and family, which often comes with consequences. Sometimes consequences are good in the long run."*

Yes, sometimes there is no other way around it, and one must be vigilant and honor what must be done no matter how ego- 'scary' it might be at times. And when what can be done, is done in a kind of naturalness without guile, the consequences become clearer, and a rarefied freshness will open more space for the spirit to breathe, at least for a while.

**A: I'll drink to that!**

Q:  Hi Lou, can you say whether the following info has any truth to it about the earth? Thanks.

Our world is hollow, with the crust of the earth being 800 miles thick.  There exist two openings at the North and South Pole, each hole having a circumference of 1400 miles wide.  At the center of the earth is not a molten core but an inner sun which is six hundred miles wide and is 2900 miles from the Inner Surfaces.  The diameter of the lip at the opening at the poles is 1200 miles long, thus a person cannot see the other side of the opening.

Therefore, there exists three worlds on our planet, the outer surface, where we live, the middle earth which purportedly is lined with many caverns, tunnels (made by someone), Inner Cities and people who live there and lastly the Inner Surface.  How Gravity works then is the following.  For the people who live on the outer surface, Gravity holds them down.  For the people that live in the middle earth, the closer they get to the center of the crust (I.e.  - 400 miles down), the less effect gravity will have upon them.

**A:  Not true but sounds like it would make for a good movie!**

# Pg. 467 — 2011-03-24

Q:  Hello Lou!!!  Here is a 5-minute video that amazes me.  It is a snapshot of future technology.  This is just what will happen with glass and doesn't include the nano technology that you speak of too.

Www.youtube.com/watch_popup?v=6Cf7IL_eZ38&vq=medium I just love watching the technology roll out.

**A:  There's a little nano behind all the 3D magic.**

Q:  Do you think Milton will be able to come and show us how all this stuff works?

**A:  Is there stale popcorn in it for him?**

Q:  Hi Lou, do aliens Joke about or make fun of us poor humans ...LOL?  And if so, could you share a joke they say about us.  Since we (humans) joke about ourselves and each other I'm sure their insight would be even funnier.  Thanks.

**A:  Shamefully it's true, they do make light of the fact that we humans only use 3 dimensions of our brain.  This video is a little funnier: [video deleted]**


Q:  **John Lear**: Listen CETI or whoever you are, I'M CALLING FROM JUPITER YOU MORON!  Get off the friggin' line.  Capisce!

**A:  Hey John, CETI could have gotten their call crossed with the king of Capisce, Joe Pesci.  Or even worse, the queen herself:  Judge Judy's Lost it – Crank Call:  https://www.youtube.com/watch?v=cHRnGbmAwPA**


Q:  Sleeper, I have to bring up the "Adjustment Bureau"  again not because it is a great or good film, but because some producer laid his reputation out on this screenplay and Matt Damon, well aware of his fifteen minutes, chose to front it.  Lots of out of the box/world intrigue disguised in this entertaining Hollywood thriller.  Maybe I am not getting a glimpse of what an ET black ops collaboration may be like???  Damn, Zarkon may just be real?

OK, everyone waste some money on this movie and rip me a new one.

**A:  Sounds like a good movie, fate with a clause, I guess I can't write the book now.**


Q:  Lou said: *"The military believes I'm an 'illegal alien' from another planet. But that's another story should I ever get around to writing it.  It's difficult not to play hooky when the weather gets nice."*

OK, just don't work as a maid or a gardener and they probably won't find you.

**A:  You mean give up my secret garden?  Never!**

Q:  Lou, Can Milton put the rumors to rest.  Was Paul McCartney killed in a 1966 car crash and replaced with a fake Beatle?  My son says hogwash.

**A:  They would have rebuilt Paul, had that been the case.  He is the real Beatle.  I need to get out more and read the tabloids, it's the first of heard of this.**


Q:  When we dream, are the people in our dreams actually there, or is it just us imagining them and creating them in our dream.

**A:  Sometimes one, sometimes the other.**


Q:  I dropped out of high school in grade 10, but that year before I dropped out, I had a class with this girl in it who I really liked and appreciated.  She liked me too, but for some reason I didn't think too much of it at the time and nothing ever happened between us.  I dropped out that year and haven't seen her since (that was 2006) 5 years ago.  She is on my Facebook, but we have never talked... haha.  I think she forgot about me probably.  Anyways, she shows up in my dreams here and there, more so lately.  I wake up and realize that I'm a weirdo for still thinking of her.  Drives me nuts sometimes.  I want to forget about it, but it always sneaks up on me.  Maybe me just thinking of what could've been?

**A:  Or she's thinking what could have been.  Sometimes there are other things going down in our dreams with people we never connect with otherwise, or not.  Many are tormented with the could have should have but are pushed and pulled in other directions by invisible busybodies.  That movie [nnnn] pointed out comes to mind**


Q:  Hi Lou.  Reading your posts brings to mind the Hank Snow song 'I've Been Everywhere'.  So, drip a little more on your impressions 'down under'.  I assume the populated places deep in the earth are not dark nor cramped.

**A:  Some are dark and cramped; there is room for a lot of things down under.**

Q:  I also assume there is no chance of humans stumbling upon such places (although books have been written about such).

**A:  Some people stumble into them and go missing.  Some forget.  Human bodies have limits to where they can go, heat, pressure, air, and all that funky stuff.**

Q:  Did you feel welcomed?

**A:  You mean with big D.**

Q:  Is the environment compatible for humans?

**A:  Mostly not.**

Q:  What did Admiral Byrd see?

**A:  He saw what he was allowed to see/remember, which has nothing to do with what he really saw.**

Q:  You have mentioned those down below can claim more ownership of the earth than us humans.  I bet they are not bothered by earthquakes and know of them well in advance...do they stop or start them?  Not asking for full disclosure, just an impression a human would get.

**A:  Nothing happens on its own, without a push here, a shove there, or a kick, for predetermined reasons, in, on and above the earth.**

## Pg. 468 — 2011-03-25

Q:  Lou said: *"With the appropriate 'prospective' we can know and understand dimensions.  Appropriate being the key."*

Hello Sleeper, you have been dropping such good drips lately I have been a bit afraid to ask some question.  Would not want Barney Doolittle the Moonshine Baron making a second appearance.  I'm kidding.

Now I had to look the word "prospective" up.  Funny never even heard that word before, I'm sure, just like always, I'll be hearing it left and right from now on though.  Now my question is about the Key to understanding dimensions, the prospective has to be appropriate....  we have to appropriately expect to understand and know dimensions?  Or we have to be appropriate to expect to know and understand dimensions?  Or our expectations whatever it may be, have to be appropriate to know and understand dimensions?

When I read your sentence my brain just overloads with the possibilities of its meaning.  The sentence is very straight forward in itself but it's no different than saying "With the right numbers "winning" the lotto you can know and understand direct depositing, numbers being the key."

I mean really, we all use it but who truly understands direct deposit?  Half the world runs off of credit, your employer uses collateral for credit to pay you, a bank giving credit to your employer sends the money to your bank, your bank counts that as a deposit, they use your deposit to give credit to an entity with collateral and the endless cycle continues, just like dimensions.  Actually, I have a feeling that understanding dimensions would be easier to understand than direct deposit.  It's not the directly depositing that's hard to understand it's the substance being deposited that is incomprehensible.

**A:  You certainly opened a whole new perspective on "direct deposits."**


Q:  Like the word "prospective" why am I going to be hearing that word left and right from now on?

**A:  Perspective is important for painters, artists and architects, and UFO nuts too, now.**

Q:  So, Sleeper is the appropriate Key to knowing and understanding dimensions, not understanding dimensions but rather expecting to see or rather experience their substance?  A perfect example.... [bad link]

You have to see for yourself to really appreciate, words fail.  Thanks Sleeper.

**A:  I'm not sure; I was distracted by the scantily dressed belly dancer.**

Q:  I was Googling New Madrid Fault for my daughter, and this popped up.  I haven't watched it all because the map was way too gloom and doom.  Sleeper, you mentioned that much of Ed Cayce's work was accurate.  He talked about this scenario.  Any drip?

**A:  I have not read much of Ed's work.**

Q:  Looks like "surfs up" for a lot of our board.  LOL!  [bad URL]

**A:  Looks more like gloom and doom, gloom, and doom.  Maybe this will cheer you up: [bad URL]**

Q:  Lou said: *"Most from here are not going to the sun, for long [time] anyway. There is no comparison between the sun and earth.  The star is a big step up."*

Are some higher ups stationed there?

**A:  Quite a few.**

Q:  Is there any secret technology or alien activity down under in the Denver international airport?

**A:  Sure, but not what most conspiracy people are claiming.  Not that I'm up on what they are claiming.**

Q: Lou said: *"Mental is too small a word to describe what is behind the magic of creation, when creation itself is only a 3D delusion.  A contradiction for the first question?  No, there are no contradictions in the real existence."*

So, creation being one of the most beautiful things but it's only a 3D delusion?

**A:  That's right.  But it's still a beautiful thing to experience.  The saying "there is nothing new under the sun" can be expanded to the universe too.  When a baby comes into our lives it's sometimes a reunion.  For some a blessed one, for some not so.  Karma either way.**

Q:  What's usually the maximum number of planets in a solar system?  Any number?  Can you reveal something that you have said anything about before?

**A:  Between none and hundreds.  Many are similar to this solar system with more than thirty.  We only know about nine.**

Q:  Have you ever witnessed exotic life forms and exotic habitats like swamps, forests etc. or any not found here on earth on other planets?  Would make a great book!

**A:  I have in my last book; the one many people believe is fiction; *A Day With An ET*.**

Q:  Dear Lou, you did start that marvelous book by saying; "Truth is a double-edged sword, to get it we must give up something—like cherished illusions."

**A:  Lies are so much easier to believe than truth.  Truth tells us things about ourselves that some of us never want to acknowledge, therefore in our minds it can't be true.  Lies tell us things we want to hear and therefore easily swallowed and followed.**

**Someone left a comment on my book at amazon.com that my book "*A Day with an ET*" is fiction and should be ignored.  Must have hit a nerve that he didn't want to acknowledge.  That book is a little fantastic and reads like**

fiction.  Perhaps it would sell if I sold it as fiction.  Nah, too much voracity and not enough sex and there's no shortage of sex.

Q:  Hey Lou, I seized upon an opportunity to rock my sister's boat the other day, well actually I thought it was more of a gentle tap, but it seems to have had the same effect as throwing a grenade into the boating lake!  She called me a bully, said some other hurtful stuff, and then basically told me to f**k off.  It was quite a humbling experience.  You were right about not everyone being ready for this info.  I should have taken more heed of your previous words to me, and now I'm just going to stick to rocking my own boat and trying to be a sturdy ladder from now on.

Lou said: *"Family, friends and invisible entities are not enough to get our personal lives in order.  Ultimately, we have to climb down into our own hellish pit, filled with vipers, old tires, gunk and who knows what else we might have dumped into it through the years.  Very little warm sunshine reaches inside the pit.  Once in the pit only personal effort and determination will get us out.  Always nice to keep a sturdy ladder handy."*

A:  **You came at her with love, she at you with hate.  I'd say you won that one hands down.  It's those little love grenades that "sometimes" makes big enough waves to make a difference somewhere down the road.  Hold your ground.**

Q:  Are items in the bible that have taken on a mythology of their own such as the "holy grail" or the "spear of destiny"  (spear of the soldier who killed Jesus) and the "sword of Michael"  the archangel, real objects like the "Ark of the covenant"  and the "tablets of destiny"  or metaphors?  Or just parts of a story that bares no relevance on their own?

A:  **Meant to be taken as real stories, and don't work well as metaphors either.  Such items have relevance only to the "fictitious" stories.  In reality, the world most of us don't want nothing to do with, such items are pure fallacy.**

Q:  And my girlfriend's family is crazy; like Dr.  Phil could do an entire season on them (she is relatively normal and a good person though), they are the complete opposite of me which is weird how we would be put together or grouped like this.  My girlfriend wants to get through to them but is that even possible?  The whole worry about what you're doing rather than saving others bit, you have said has proved to be quite true for me with recent experiences.

Thanks.

A:  **None of us have the power to save others, only the power to save ourselves.  Most people are not even aware they have such power for themselves but think they do with others.**

**When meddling with others they "always" assume the meddler is looking down on them as inferior – even when that may not be the case.  Helping others can be a minefield and can sometimes do more damage than good.  Especially those who are dragged down into the mud of hate and become hateful and resentful themselves.  Happens all the time to amateurs and experts.**

## Pg. 469 — 2011-03-28

Q:  Lou said: *"Many are similar to this solar system with more than thirty."*

**John Lear**: WHAT?!!!  OMIGOD!!!!!

A: **"Give a man enough rope and he will eventually hang himself with it".  As you know, John, when Galileo expanded on Copernicus' theory concerning the planets and their movement around the sun, the clergy threw him under the heretic bus.  But unlike heretics before him he was not burnt at the stake but was confined to his villa and told to shut up.**

**As you know, back then it was Science verses King-of-the-hill Religion, religion won, and much time passed before science gained a foothold and some respectability.  Now Science is king of the hill and this UFO nut the heretic.  Pregnant suns and planets out the wazoo are not only insane ideas**

but downright blasphemous to the institutions whose foundations rely on blind obedience to Mr. and Mrs. status quo.

Science is doing exactly what religion did a few hundred years ago, constipating the works that don't suit them.  Yeah, it's all part of the grand design.  Oh, and where's the proof to pregnant suns and all those extra planetary mouths to feed?  As in Galileo's case, proof happens slowly and over time; it causes violent rocking of the boat making people sick.


Q:  Holy universal drips!!!  30 planets?!!!!!!!!  LOU!!!!!!!!!  That's about a good excuse as any… DROAD TRIP!!!!!!!!!!!!  weeeeeeeeeee.

A:  The stale popcorn done Milty in, he doesn't look road trip worthy.  I can't fill in! I get lost whenever I go to the mall with the wife.


Q:  Hello Lou, yesterday I watched a documentary about a scholar who theorized that most NT stories about Jesus, were in fact based upon the stories of Julius Caesar (JC).  The resemblances really were uncanny.  JC was considered a son of God (Venus).  He travelled from Gaulle (Galilei) to the holy city.  The names of the people around JC resemble the names mentioned in the NT.  A wax copy of Julius Caesar's stabbed body was even nailed onto a cross to show the people of Rome how he died.  And beneath the exact center of St. Peters Cathedral in Rome is the family tomb of the Julii family.

Can you ask Milton if the biography of Julius Caesar did indeed serve as a prototype in creating the myth of Jesus Christ?  Thanks.

A:  No doubt some of Caesar's material ended up in the salad mix.  Many writers use popular concepts of the time already on people's minds, overlapping them and making them more believable stories.  But much of the Jesus story is taken from the old testament books and given new appropriate to the day twists, by "people" extremely familiar with Jewish literature and customs like the Jewish sect the Essenes.

Jesus broke every Jewish rule, law, and custom in those books, that's why few Jews converted to Christianity, they understood the fallacy behind the story, things non-Jews failed to catch or understand.

Q: Holy shit Lou, 30+ planets!! Now that's the mother of all drips! Can't wait for the follow up queries and drips.

I'll kick off with this one: are any of the undiscovered planets in orbit between the sun and Jupiter?

**A: Some are further out, past Pluto the dwarf planet. Others closer in.**

Q: I think Lou has said there are planets hidden or invisible (to us) right close to earth. There could be a whole planet(s) of aliens just watching us within sight of earth that we have no idea about...LOL.

Hi Lou, what did the Tablets of Destiny of Sumerian lore do? Thanks.

**A: They would have made good paper weights, had there been paper.**

## Pg. 470 — 2011-03-29

Q: Sleeper, I remember you saying that ET camouflaged some places in our Solar system, but 30 or so....whoah! Planets? Are you including the babies that are barely visible? Or the babies taken out of our solar system?

**A: The solar system is a tad larger than is currently known. The sun spits faster than humans and their toy telescopes blink and deposits things out in the boonies regularly, planets too.**

Q: Hell, I'm still trying to formulate questions about the big cruise ships...any drip on those?

**A: Yes, they pickup tourists and depart punctually. Make reservations far in advance – they pack up fast.**

Q:  Just watched a Pompeii documentary...Pliny, the Elder's son's record of the blast was scoffed at by scientists until Mt.  St.  Helens did the same thing...LOL! Oooo, quick rewrite the textbooks again.

A:  **A shame they don't give out Nobel awards for scientific scoffing.**


Q:  Was Pompeii a clean-up or just your run of the mill Terra catastrophe?

A:  **Pompeii is a snapshot of Roman life two thousand years ago.  Some pictures are worth a few thousand lives.  We all must die to make room for other inmates. Yes on clean-up.**


Q:  I'd like your thoughts on a topic that recently came up.

I experience substantial difficulties with disrespect – this is especially true for people I allow myself to become close with.  Given that I do what I can to "walk the karma line", so to speak.  Apply as much positivity to life as I can and hold myself responsible for everything that happens around me.  I typically apologize first for any negative situations, despite my understanding of the other person's clearly inappropriate behavior.  When that person refuses to accept or acknowledge their behavior, and doesn't reciprocate with their own apology, that creates an incredibly difficult challenge for me.

A:  **Whenever we set up "expectations" from others, we will "always" be disappointed and frustrated.  No getting around that elephant no matter how righteous we might be feeling at any given moment.**

**Those deserving respect don't reside on this planet.  Those expecting respect do.**


Q:  On one hand, I feel positive knowing that I didn't lose control and say or act in a way that would have drastically worsened the conversation, and I can feel confident knowing that I've taken the appropriate steps in my own life and my own path, and that's clearly important for me and my soul.  However, that positivity is completely overshadowed by the extreme negativity I begin to feel related to the disrespect expressed by the other person – this negativity usually lasts a couple of days, and then I begin to come out of it.

**A:  Whenever someone disrespects you why heap more coals on your own head by stewing over it?  Either punch the mother__er in the mouth and move on, or let it slide and move on.**

Q:  After that type of incident occurs, I typically take measures to protect myself and prevent that from occurring between the other person and myself again – this usually entails a complete reevaluation of our relationship, and either completely changing my behavior in respect to that person, or stopping my association with that person altogether (that hasn't happened often, however, it's felt necessary in the past).  The reasoning behind discontinuing my association with certain folks was that in order to be the best person I can to the people around me, my friends, and family, I have to maintain a positive and healthy state of mind – otherwise, I'm no good to anyone.  So, as much as I understand that it's not the most positive approach to take.  It's felt like the only available option and interestingly enough, still feels like the appropriate step to have taken (for incidents that have already taken place, that is).  With that said, when I have discontinued my association with someone, it was never after something I felt guilty or responsible for, nor was it a huge catastrophic incident.  I just thought and reasoned after the incident(s) and concluded that it'd be best for both the other person and me.

**A:  The problem is never simple to solve.  The more something or someone gets on our nerves the more it tends to increase.  Like flies on a pile of warm poop.  Confront and conquer or submit and get over it.  Most people, family and friends included, are not in our lives to make us comfortable.  Well some are.**

**Life challenges us and roots out hidden weaknesses in every niche in our soul.  It's a painful and humiliating process most of the time.**

Q:  It's worth mentioning that those situations happen less and less frequently in my life (the last time was work related over last summer, and then again last night) so, it's fair to expect that I'm growing and improving.  However, I'm still trying to understand where all of this fits in, and what I can do to prevent either the incidents themselves or the negativity that I feel afterward.  Thanks in advance for any feedback.

**A:  Some people choose violence and anger in those types of situations. Sometimes works for a while but the beast only gets bigger and hungrier and will have to be dealt with at some point before a soul can move forward.**

**No one wants or handles disrespect and humiliation well.  But the gods favor those methods the most.  It's a test after all.**

## Pg. 471 — 2011-03-30

Q:  Lou said: "*Hi, [nnnn].  You came at her with love, she at you with hate.  I'd say you won that one hands down.  It's those little love grenades that "sometimes" make big enough waves to make a difference somewhere down the road.  Hold your ground.*"

I really needed to hear this Lou; I was starting to have serious doubts about what I was doing.  But neither my Sister nor anyone else can convince me that swallowing pride, letting go of anger, hatred and bitterness is wrong.  I know that it is easier said than done in certain very challenging situations, I am still struggling with my feelings for my Dad, but one step at a time I think, miracles don't happen overnight...well, sometimes they do ...LOL, but...

My Sister is hiding behind pride and fear which I can totally relate to.  I have to tread carefully with her; she's very fragile and not ready to face her demons yet, but hopefully like you said, somewhere down the road she will have a change of heart.  I will hold my ground.

Lou, from the bottom of my heart, thank you so, so much!

**A:  For good measure, why not throw her a love grenade from [nnnn] and the gang.  As bizarre as it sounds some people enjoy stewing in anger.  There is a certain perverted pleasure derived from it, especially if they get lots of attention for their theatrics.  And they "hate" to admit it.  Fortunately, some people eventually grow up.**

Q: Quick one: Dinosaurs....many different species and eras...were some of them (the most popular Sue types) sentient – as in tech savvy, cultural?  Souls?  Or just animal instinct?  Pets for?

**A:  Ego gone wild and over the top.  Dino's were/are used for entertainment, terror, and a few other things not appropriate to speak about in a family friendly UFO nut site.**

Q:  Hello Lou, Thank you very much for 3000 awesome posts.  Do submarines travel from the Pacific, under the Rockies to Nevada?  Thanks again

**A:  That's crazy talk, we don't do that around here (crazy talk). Well, sometimes.**

Q:  Lou said: *"Those deserving respect don't reside on this planet.  Those expecting respect do."*

Heya Lou!  As soon as we start entertaining conceptual distinctions about who is worthy and who isn't, aren't we also establishing conditions for greed, hatred, envy, and delusion?  Blessings!

**A:  Yes, that's why no one down here merits respect, not even me, John and the pope, to name a few.  We all want to be respected, and for my daily dose of respect I go to McDonald's or Wall Mart and other such places, where people are "paid" to shower you with respect (employees instructed in being courteous to customers).  Nevertheless, it sure does feel good.**

**Avoid government agencies like tax offices, water departments and the car license bureau, they show no respect and treat you like cattle.**

Q:  Lou said: *"Jesus broke every Jewish rule and custom in those books, that's why few Jews converted to Christianity, they understood the fallacy behind the story, things non-Jews failed to catch or understand."*

Hola Sleeper!  I just finished reading *"Shrouded Chronicles of Jesus the Christ"* - it's a good read, and I recognized a lot of answers to questions here on Message

Board are in it, nice!  The Essenes "brought" the new message.  Were they working close with ET to help write the coded message?

A:  **The Essenes and some other sects wrote many books, most never made the final cut.  ET's did reside among the people back then, and now, and forever.**

Q:  pg. 47 "Freewill has given us that choice: to live apart from our maker or abide with him, an option all demons have taken and must live with" - demons can't take that choice back/ repent?  We / our souls are or were not those demons, were we?

A:  **Hell no!!!**

Q:  pg. 54 "ESP, thought to be a modern scientific discovery is in fact an ancient form of prayer.  Astrology, Seance, Witchcraft or Tarot Cards are used in contacting anything outside the physical realm.  It's not how we communicate, it's who we communicate with that makes us what we are spiritually and physically" - So (the bible) this message board is an opportunity/tool to switch ESP service providers so we can upgrade ourselves spiritually and physically?

A:  **Yeah, but we don't have two-year lock-in plans in exchange for free phones.**

Q:  The idea or new way of "Jesus" broke all rules the Hebrew/Jewish nation followed.  Was this new idea based on the only constant, Karma?  Thanks in advance.

A:  **Everything is based on karma.  The character Jesus "literally" broke all Jewish traditions and laws (easy to do when you are only a figment of someone's imagination, like creating a superhero).  Such blatant disregard "always" came with immediate condemnation by the high priests, stoning and death rapidly followed. And no figment about that.**

Q:  **John Lear**: Lou, [nnnn] means the Sierra Nevada.  The Rocky Mountains are in a slightly different location.

A:  **Thanks for that John!  Seriously, I wouldn't know my Rocky Mountains from my Sierra Nevada's.  I need to get out more.**


Q:  I have an easy question for you.  I have been wondering if there is any truth to the idea or technique of "manifestations", for lack of a better word, (not dem bug manifestations) ……

I think you may have briefly touched on this.  It's the concept of bringing into one's life a desired effect.

As per example in the book 'The Secret'.  So, say, one wants to have a new car, one intently focuses on that and eventually magically it comes.  So there any truth to that?

A:  **There is truth to that.  Mostly it is pre-negotiated, we easily forget those prebirth negotiations.**


Q:  Can one "will" something materially 'good' into their lives, not based on greed or negative desires?

A:  **There is always a catch – being that few, if any of us down here do anything without an element of greed and negative desires.  Come on, how much fun can we have without a bit of dark side mixed in with our daily coffee.**


Q:  If it can be done, is there a karmic price for that?  Thank you very much for your drips.

A:  **Nothing is free!  Not even a free lunch.  Nevertheless, we are allowed indulgences without consequences.  Considering that most, already have everything their souls desire hidden away somewhere waiting for them. Getting a taste of the good life now and then is encouraged.  The good life is**

**the only reality in existence, everything else is illusion, painful illusion, but nonetheless, illusion...with an expiration date.**

Q:  Hello Lou, you remarked the Beatles came in with free passes.  Does that mean they are not/weren't prisoners on this planet?  Although I am a massive Beatles fan, I have to say I never had them down as people who didn't have the usual human flaws.  Those who were close to them have said as much.  You might even say that a little bit of hate, envy and greed finally drove them apart.  I take it John was shot because he'd dished out the same somewhere down the line (?) and though it maybe karma for him to mull over, Julian Lennon has been quite blunt about John Lennon's shortcomings as a dad.

A:  **A free pass means they got to play demigods for a time as do most celebrities.  It doesn't mean you are free from human suffering/baggage and pitfalls.  Heck, if they were free from such some of us would think they really were gods.  Once they die the shine comes off and they face the same trial Judges everyone else faces, perhaps more.**

Q:  Anyways, on a quite different note I keep meaning to ask you for your view on the growing earth theory.  It posits that the earth was once smaller, without the major oceans.  The argument against is that it cannot be explained scientifically, which is not an argument in my view, because you shouldn't deny things just because you can't explain them.

Neal Adams – Science: 01 – Conspiracy: Earth is Growing!

https://www.youtube.com/watch?time_continue=1&v=oJfBSc6e7QQ

A:  **Earth was much smaller, and the oceans added much later.  The Earth was smaller than Mercury and naked.  Earth and the other planets did "Not" form from an accretion disk of material.  The prevailing theory is "WRONG".**

Q:  Hi Lou and John.  I have a question about déjà vu.  I know that it is a remnant of a disruption but what I have experienced is a feeling that washes over me and the realization that I have done and or have been here before. Almost like I had dreamt about it, not a feeling of lost time – more like stepping into the situation from another time?

It's hard to accurately describe the feeling because it has not happened since I was young. The sensation was of immediate recognition that I had done these exact things before, like watching a film of the event. In a way I kind of miss the experience – it made me feel special.

**A:  When we get "disrupted" our essence sometimes spills over the time-line mostly on purpose. When that happens, we do live that frame/section over again. Déjà vu happens anytime, anywhere, even when people are all around us. Disruptions and the "vu" don't necessarily happen in conjunction, mostly they don't.**

## Pg. 472 — 2011-03-31

Q:  Lou said: *"...no one down here merits respect ..."*

I don't know, Lou. I'd say respect simply means treating others the way we would have others treat us. In that case, everyone and everything is worthy of respect, since we are all inextricably connected in consciousness. That is love.

On the other hand, since everything appearing (including our self-image – who we imagine ourselves to be) is of the same nature as an illusion, a dream, a dew drop, a falling star, a flash of light in a dark infinity, it would be unskillful to identify with any of it, but wiser to stand aloof and dispassionate, even in the midst of the daily staged carnage passing for life on earth these days. One fellow summed it up this way:

*"When I see I am everything, that is love.*

*When I see I am nothing, that is wisdom.*

*Between these two, my life flows."*

I also like this one, from the LongchenpA:

*"Since everything is but an apparition, having nothing to do with good or bad, acceptance or rejection, one may well burst out in laughter."*

A:  True, but respect is not something you tattoo on your arm.  Those deserving of respect "never" seek it – those who seek it never have it.  Being nice and friendly is "not" respect, its being nice and friendly.  People "respect": authority, the powerful, the gangsta, the institutions.  It's all semantics – the crowd you hang with determines the meaning of words.  Words are given new meaning all the time.  The world is spiraling forever into a New Babylon of "self-interest" groups with their own lingo.

Q:  I wanted to ask if NASA has ever seen things on Mars via the rovers that will NEVER be revealed to the public (and made their hair stand up).  If you say no, I'll be surprised.... again.

A:  NASA sees things that makes their hair stand up every day, that's why they are not talking.  They don't know how to put into words what they see.  Yeah on Mars too.

Q:  When did the Moon appear in Earth orbit?

A:  On a moonless night when the wolves had nothing to howl about.

Q:  Greetings Lou, is it possible to multitask on higher levels (Utopia+) and explore lot of things at once?  Like watch movie + travel + party + study + read book etc., all at once?  Right now, we have to choose here on earth how to invest our time and attention, and it's not cool.

A:  Yes, it's a whole lot easier to multitask when not chewing gum.  No gum up there.

Q:  On Utopia level, what kind of entertainment is awaiting us?  Do they "watch TV" or read books, any sport activities, or playing "video" games?

A:  Everything they do is entertainment, never a dull moment or bad hair day, never.

Q:  Could you give us a short example what a typical day for someone in Utopia looks like?  Warm regards.

A:  **Like a relaxing massage by sweet cute angels.  I gave an example in my "A Day with an ET" documentary/book.**

## Pg. 473 — 2011-04-02

Q:  Lou, after we die, do we go to the sun, then are sent somewhere else from there?

A:  **Some do, some don't.  It's all in the condition souls are in.**

Q:  Lou, thanks again.  30 planets?  Is this in our density/space time channel but cloaked except for the mostly out past Pluto ones?

A:  **Yes and no.  There is a whole lot of stuff not cloaked floating all over this inner solar system.  Granted some of it is camouflaged.  There is so much space and not enough eyes to see but a fraction of what is going on. Some types of mass don't disturb other types of mass.**

Q:  Is our sun connected to a larger orbit, i.e., do we orbit a bigger central star? Have read that so many times?

A:  **No.**

Q:  Is there no possibility in the future of various races getting along, I.e., having read of the Lacerta Files: www.luisprada.com/Protected/the_lacerta_files.htm

A:  **You mean like human races get along?**

Q:  Surely systems where it's all possible.  Do not systems upgrade for example or only souls?

**A: Systems exist to serve souls.**

Q: And this silly question that nonetheless keeps bugging me. So many use the word "cookies" or "cookies and milk". And I never believe they are talking about real cookies. Are they talking about programming people with digital cookies? Or one conversation was about stealing cookies, a whole train of thought for me. Should we be guarding our cookies? LOL.

**A: Are we talking chocolate chip? If so, heck yes!**


Q: Hi Lou & others! I've found a very interesting documentary. There is this guy at 5:00 who is telling a similar thing as you according to some ancient writings called Vedas. Check it out.

UFO SECRET: Alien Contacts – FEATURE FILM: https://www.youtube.com/watch?v=L9nB2NxQ9XU Sorry for my bad English but I think he says something like this:

Richard Thomson – Sanskrit Scholar

"According to the Vedic literature there are many different types of human-like beings living in the universe and they are all descendant from an original common ancestor. According to the Vedic writings there has been communications between human beings and other types of human like beings throughout the universe for thousands and thousands of years. This used to be in fact more common than it is now. According to the Vedic literature we are now in a period called "Kali Yuga?" in which communication between humans and higher forms of life is somewhat curtailed. So, the idea is this communication was much more extensive in the past.

Well the ultimate question of purpose boils down to the question of what is the ultimate purpose of life why did this universe come to be in the first place? The basic concept that you have in the Vedic literature, starting in the middle basically of the explanation is that you have living beings who have spirits souls – the soul is the essence of the being who are in a state of ignorance. These living beings are situated in bodies made of material elements and because of this these material bodies don't understand the true nature of the self. So, there is an evolutionary process whereby, through experience in the material world in different material bodies one can gradually elevate one's consciousness. So, life on Earth also is a school which living beings take bodies of human form on the Earth to undergo certain experiences, which in do-course, will elevate their consciousness.  So, the purpose of communication from higher beings in the universe **is to aid in this process**.  To give people instructions which will ultimately enable them to attain a higher level of consciousness.

So the idea is that on the Earth people are basically living in the state of ignorance but from time to time beings from the higher systems within the universe will come down to the Earth and transmit spiritual knowledge to the people here on Earth.  So in this way you have different religions developing, of course that's a very complex process because once knowledge is transmitted to this Earth then people begin to do things without knowledge and so you can have the development of different religious creations, etc."

**A:  About twenty years ago a man named George Adamski called me on the telephone, not the George Adamski of UFO lore, who had died many years earlier.  This Adamski wanted me to build him a house.  He was an engineer at the Ford plant and had seen some of my houses or builder signs in the area, he said.  I met with him at his house, a large beautiful new house in an upper bracket subdivision on three acres.  It made no sense that he should want a new house in the same area.  I met him a few times at this office at the Ford plant (Claycomo, MO.) to go over house plans.  The deal fell through when he came to my house to go over details about the house he wanted to build.  He pointed out the "foreign" car in the driveway, my wife's, and said that was a deal breaker.  Never saw him after that.**

**I haven't read any of Adamski's books or looked into his UFO contacts and claims; I wasn't into UFO nuts back then.  I was aware of my own sporadic contacts but never talked about them to anyone.  Something during my meetings with Adamski triggered things that eventually lead to my meeting with other beings that opened more info for my first book, In League with a UFO, a few years later.  It's been all downhill from there.** lol

**[I've never heard of or read the Vedic literature or most other books concerning Aliens and UFOs and the mysteries of humans and beings from the stars in various nations and cultures. I was a home builder and uninterested in such stuff.]**

## Pg. 474 — 2011-04-05 thru Pg. 490 — 2011-06-05

Q:  Hi sleeper long time no talk; tell Milton I said hello; I still seem to be pulling some sort of duty at night; an RV session with a friend says I am working with a group she calls the rangers and supposedly from Andromeda?  I know I wake up tired as hell most mornings, any thoughts?

A:  **You are tired from that long commute!  Andromeda?  I don't think so. But pulling long hard night shifts in the salt mines right here in our solar system is common.  Someone must dig out the salt, for what is life without a little flavor?**

**BTW, I don't answer questions here much, mostly at this site for now:** www.ufolou.com

Q:  Lou, does the prime creator (God (NOT CHRISTIAN)) exist?

A:  **No "prime creator," a concept far too difficult for the 3D mind to comprehend, like the idea of no time and everything being illusion.**

**BTW, I'm locking "this thread" for now.  The rest of this board, forum, is open and new topics can be added.**

## Pg. 490 — 2011-06-05

End of Thread

# BOOKS BY THE AUTHOR

1. In League with a UFO Second Edition (177pg.)1997
2. Shrouded Chronicles (267 pg.) ......................2000
3. A Day with an Extraterrestrial (159 pg.) ........2006
4. An Italian Family, Capisce? (197 pg.) ..............2011
5. Israel Crucified (215 pg.) ...................................2012
6. Orphans of Aquarius (209 pg.) ......................2012
7. UFOs in the Year of the Dragon (217 pg.) .......2012
8. Mars and the lost planet Man (215 pg.) ..........2014
9. Graduation into the Cosmos (203 Pg.) ............2016
10. Planet Eropmanop (253 pg.) ............................2017
11. Alien hybrids and nymphs of Jupiter (207 pg.)2019

**BLOGS IN BOOK FORM**

UFOs and Extraterrestrials are as real as the nose on your face Blog, 2005... Published in book form, 2011 (383 pg.)

Coming clean on Extraterrestrials and the UFO Hidden Agenda...Blog, 2007-8

(357 pg.) Part 1...2011

(329 pg.) Part 2...2012

(303 pg.) Part 3...2012

(329 pg.) Part 4...2012

(291 pg.) Part 5...2013

(351 pg.) Part 6...2013

EXTRATERRESTRIAL SPEAK PART ONE (347 pg.)   2015

EXTRATERRESTRIAL SPEAK BOOK TWO (277 pg.)  2016

EXTRATERRESTRIAL SPEAK PART THREE (261 pg.) 2019

EXTRATERRESTRIAL SPEAK PART FOUR (355 pg.)  2019

EXTRATERRESTRIAL SPEAK PART FIVE (249 pg.)    2019

EXTRATERRESTRIAL SPEAK PART SIX (217 pg.)      2019

EXTRATERRESTRIAL SPEAK PART SEVEN (273 pg.) 2020

EXTRATERRESTRIAL SPEAK PART EIGHT (220 pg.)  2020

EXTRATERRESTRIAL SPEAK PART NINE (212 pg.)    2020

EXTRATERESTRIAL SPEAK PART TEN (113 pg.)       2020


## Websites

ufolou.com

baldin.proboards.com

FACEBOOK. Lou Baldini

www.ingramcontent.com/pod-product-compliance
Lightning Source LLC
Chambersburg PA
CBHW010424120726
47992CB00008B/3324